A WALK IN THE PARK

A WALK IN THE PARK

Greater Cleveland's New and Reclaimed Green Spaces

DIANA TITTLE

with ParkWorks

Photographs by Janet Century

Ohio University Press

Athens

Ohio University Press, Athens, Ohio 45701
© 2002 by Ohio University Press
Printed in Canada
All rights reserved

Ohio University Press books are printed on acid-free paper ⊗ ™

10 09 08 07 06 05 04 03 02   5 4 3 2 1

Library of Congress Cataloging-in-Publication Data

Tittle, Diana, 1950–
     A walk in the park : greater Cleveland's new and reclaimed green spaces /
Diana Tittle with ParkWorks.
        p. cm.
     Includes bibliographical references (p.).
     ISBN 0-8214-1406-2
     1. Urban parks—Ohio—Cleveland Region—History. 2. Parks—Ohio—
Cleveland Region—History. 3. Cleveland Region (Ohio)—History, Local.
4. Cleveland Region (Ohio)—Description and travel. 5. City planning—Ohio—
Cleveland Region—History. I. ParkWorks. II. Title.

     F499.C672 T58 2001
     977.1'32—dc21
                                                    2001034635

CONTENTS

Preface   vii

Acknowledgments xi

1   Introduction: The Good Fight:
     A Brief History of Parks Activism and
     Advocacy in Greater Cleveland

12   Lincoln Park: The People's Commons

21   Fine Arts Garden: A Place to Remember

31   Ohio & Erie Canal Reservation:
     Observing Nature at Work

41   Mill Creek Falls Park & Trail:
     Pathway to Revitalization

53   Hershey Children's Garden:
     Play That Educates

63   Forest Hills Park:
     Programmed to Succeed

72   Cleveland Lakefront State Park:
     Back in the Swim

81   Rockefeller Park: The Value of Networking

90   Cleveland Cultural Gardens:
      A Place to Remember, Part Two

98   Cleveland's New Elementary School
      Playgrounds: Springboards for Change

106   Eastman Reading Garden:
      A Bit of Heaven

116   Cuyahoga Valley National Park:
      Preserving the Panorama of the Past
      Twelve Thousand Years

128   Mentor Lagoons Nature Preserve
      and Marina: A Miraculous Save

140   Upper Doan Valley Parklands:
      Restoring "God's Pleasure"

151   Epilogue: Envisioning a Brighter,
      Greener Future

Further Reading   161

Contents

PREFACE

We Greater Clevelanders are not inclined to take our blessings for granted. We saved the Browns, remodeled Severance Hall, restructured the governance of our public schools. We have made progress toward rebuilding our central-city neighborhoods and cleaning up Lake Erie and the Cuyahoga River. Now we are renewing our longstanding fight for more and better green spaces. This book documents both the history and the current round of that battle.

The terminology of combat is chosen deliberately. The struggle to preserve, enlarge, and enhance the region's parklands has been, and will continue to be, titanic. The enemy (as Pogo, the Walt Kelly comic strip character, says) is us, or at least our general heedlessness of ever-expanding urban development. Sprawl chews up farmlands and wild areas—potential parklands and natural oases—while undermining the ability of our core communities to maintain quality public services, including the care and improvement of their existing green spaces.

In profiling fourteen parks and green spaces located throughout the Greater Cleveland area—beloved community assets that have been either saved or created over the past twenty-five years with the help of "average" citizens—this book offers reason for cautious optimism. More and more people are saying No! to the status quo. Taken as a whole, these stories of renewal and innovation demonstrate the grass-roots strength and gathering momentum of Greater Cleveland's regional parks movement. ParkWorks, the book's sponsor, and the other underwriters listed in the acknowledgments have stepped forward to share this good news in the hope of inspiring greater public advocacy and activism on behalf of parks among all members of the community, including Greater Cleveland's most influential citizens, who have provided exceptional leadership in this arena in the past. There is far more good to be achieved.

Greater Cleveland's parks proponents are now poised to embellish our rightly famed Emerald Necklace. They have conceived, and have obtained federal seed money to begin building, an interconnected network of green spaces that will re-energize every section of the region. Like its cyberspace equivalent, the emerging regional parks network has the potential to boost our economy and enrich the daily lives of every man, woman, and child—rich or poor, black, white, or Hispanic—living here. As this ambitious plan has, to date, received only limited public attention, the final chapter of this book is devoted to painting the "big picture" and discussing the life-altering possibilities that accompany a greener future. An understanding of the prospects for improvement will surely build support for greater public investment in the creation, reclamation, and linkage of parks and green spaces throughout the region.

The open spaces profiled in this book are among the chief building blocks of Greater Cleveland's emerging regional parks network. They range from playgrounds and pocket parks through neighborhood and community parks to state and federal parklands and nature preserves. Something these diverse recreational resources have in common is that each has been created—or, in the case of older parks, rescued from neglect and disuse—by neighborhood residents and passionate constituents acting in concert with concerned public officials and civic leaders.

This book names and applauds these unsung heroes for their vision, ingenuity, and perseverance. It also explains, in broad outline, how the featured public-private partnerships achieved these "miracles" of urban renascence (as one of the principals rightly terms park-building efforts). These descriptions are intended to help those seeking to reclaim their own neighborhood and community parks or to create new green spaces. In the aggregate the profiles provide an overview of the objectives, action steps, techniques, and resources of park-building work.

If nothing else, the book's underwriters hope to motivate Greater Clevelanders to get up off their couches, grab the kids, and head for the parks featured in these pages. To encourage greater patronage of these wonderful spaces, each profile invites readers to experience the unique charms of a particular park, delight in its distinctive ambiance and amenities, and discover its fascinating history. Ending on a more reflective note, each profile highlights a specific contribution that parks can make to societal well-being. These explorations cover endeavors as diverse as leisure and ecology . . . education and historic preservation . . . habitat conservation and community building . . . and scientific research and economic development.

Yes, it may come as a surprise that parks, which some people associate exclusively with fresh air and fun, can have a much wider-ranging socioeconomic impact.

A brief summary of the many benefits that can be derived from abundant parks and open spaces would start with something fairly obvious: their promotion of physical fitness. (This is a topic that should be of special concern in Greater Cleveland, which ranks fifth in the nation in the percentage of its adult inhabitants who are obese, according to the National Center for Health Statistics.) By providing no-cost places in which to exercise, parks can enable people to lead longer, more productive lives.

Green spaces make for healthier communities, too. They provide venues for celebrations and festivals, fostering a sense of solidarity and civility among people from all walks of life. They offer recreational outlets for youngsters, contributing to decreases in vandalism and crime. As proven focal points for real estate development and commercial growth, they promote neighborhood reinvestment and renewal. And as the "lungs" of our urban areas, they clean and cool the air and safeguard our water sources, reducing the need for costly environmental remediation and mechanical infrastructures.

As engines of economic development, parks are truly powerful. They can burnish the image of a city or a region more effectively than a multimillion-dollar advertising campaign. A visible measure of an excellent quality of life, they have the potential to attract new and relocating businesses, thus creating jobs and economic opportunity. Green spaces also draw tourists, whose presence can stimulate the start-up of related businesses and services. Local property owners fortunate enough to have acquired land adjoining open space or a well-functioning park benefit from the enhanced marketability and value of their holdings. And higher property values mean stronger municipal tax bases, which can translate into new and improved public services.

In short, parks are clearly much more than dedicated spaces for public swimming pools and swing sets. They can be the heart and soul of a community. "In order for a city to be vibrant, for a downtown to be vibrant, you have to have great neighborhoods," ParkWorks executive director Ann Zoller states. "And you can't have great neighborhoods without great parks."

This is an account of the progress we Greater Clevelanders have made toward achieving that ideal.

Diana Tittle

ACKNOWLEDGMENTS

The publication of this book has been made possible by the generous support of Cleveland Metroparks, the Cuyahoga Valley National Park, and the Cleveland Public Library, as well as by grants from The Cleveland Foundation and The George Gund Foundation.

Additional underwriting was provided by Behnke & Associates, The Church in the City Program of The Diocese of Cleveland, the Cleveland Museum of Natural History, Davey Tree, the city of Mentor, the Northeast Ohio Regional Sewer District, Schmidt Copeland Parker Stevens, Slavic Village Development Corporation, Sustainable Communities 2000, and The Trust for Public Land.

Personal acknowledgment is also owed to ParkWorks Director of Program Development Barbara Clint, the book's project manager, and to the following individuals both for their roles in securing the financial participation of their respective institutions in this project and for the ongoing vision and leadership they have provided to Greater Cleveland's expanding network of parks, gardens, and green spaces:

Vern J. Hartenburg, Executive Director and Secretary, Cleveland Metroparks

John Debo, Superintendent, Cuyahoga Valley National Park

Andrew A. Venable, Director, Cleveland Public Library

Robert Jacquay, Associate Director, The George Gund Foundation

Robert E. Eckardt, Senior Program Officer, The Cleveland Foundation

Jim Bissell, Curator of Botany and Natural Areas, Cleveland Museum of Natural History

Elizabeth L. Buchanan, Manager of Biological Services, Davey Tree

Julian M. Suso, City Manager, City of Mentor

Erwin J. Odeal, Executive Director, Northeast Ohio Regional Sewer District

Christopher D. Knopf, Ohio Field Office Director, The Trust for Public Land

Patty Stevens, Schmidt Copeland Parker Stevens

Sister Rita Mary Harwood, SND, The Church in the City Program of The Diocese of Cleveland

Phil Hart, Chairman, Sustainable Communities 2000

Tom Zarfoss, Chairman, Behnke Associates, Inc.

Bobbi Reichtell, Development Manager, Slavic Village Development Corporation

A WALK IN THE PARK

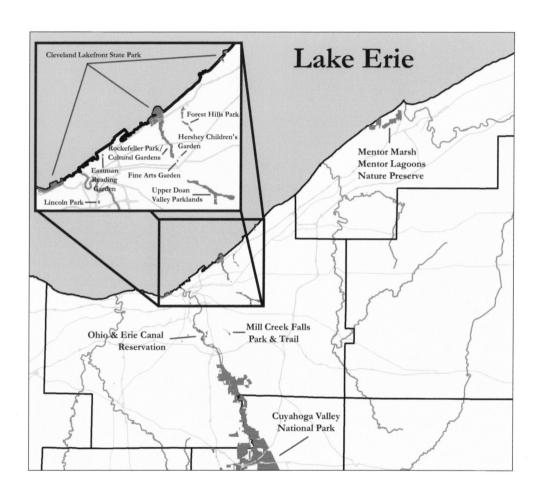

Lake Erie

Cleveland Lakefront State Park

Forest Hills Park

Hershey Children's Garden

Rockefeller Park/ Cultural Gardens

Eastman Reading Garden

Fine Arts Garden

Lincoln Park

Upper Doan Valley Parklands

Mentor Marsh Mentor Lagoons Nature Preserve

Ohio & Erie Canal Reservation

Mill Creek Falls Park & Trail

Cuyahoga Valley National Park

INTRODUCTION

The Good Fight

A BRIEF HISTORY OF PARKS ACTIVISM AND ADVOCACY IN GREATER CLEVELAND

On July 22, 1796, Moses Cleaveland paced off the boundaries of a ten-acre commons in a proposed new settlement in the Connecticut Western Reserve. Historians tell us that Cleaveland was laying out the settlement's communal grazing grounds, following a design that had become traditional in his native New England. But the generous size of the commons and the gracious, twelve-foot width of the avenues that were to bisect it suggest that Cleaveland intended the square to serve a much grander purpose. Perhaps he was thinking of Boston Commons, Colonial America's first known park, when he placed a public gathering place at the heart of his envisioned "capital" of the Western Reserve.

Moses Cleaveland, the leader of an expedition sent to the Western Reserve to survey and map the holdings of the Connecticut Land Company, was a graduate of Yale, a Revolutionary War officer, and a lawyer—in short, a man of refinement. It was to be expected that such a person would wish to design a capital city that would serve both commerce (thus the settlement's location at the mouth of the Cuyahoga River on Lake Erie) *and* culture (thus the spacious public square at its center).

If Cleaveland seems to have been something of an urban planner, the leaders who followed him, though capable, were blind to the advantages of and need for additional open space in the city named for Cleaveland that grew up around Public Square. Their eyes were focused on the pursuit of commerce. Abetted by the construction of the Ohio & Erie Canal, the rise of Great Lakes shipping, and the coming of the railroads, they transformed a malaria-plagued agricultural village into a major mercantile and transportation center. With a population that stood at 92,000 in 1870, Cleveland—the first "a" was dropped from the name early on—had indeed become the dominant city in northeast Ohio. Clevelanders (or at least those of some means) enjoyed access to street lights, water and sewer service, newspapers, theater performances, libraries, and hospitals. Yet, nearly a century after Public Square had been laid out, the city fathers had seen fit to create no other *public* spaces. Moses Cleaveland's "city on a hill" had become a dense, suffocating warren.

Ignoring press and popular opinion alike, Cleveland City Council had turned down several opportunities to purchase land for parks in the center of a city that had seen its population skyrocket during the canal-boom days. (In 1830 Cleveland had 1,075 inhabitants; by 1860 the population stood at 43,417.) Deprived of alternative venues in which to enjoy the open air, Clevelanders pleaded with council to cordon off Public Square so that they could stroll there without having to dodge horse carts and carriages. Between 1857 and 1867 a double-railed white fence enclosed the grounds, but the effort to protect Public Square's integrity as a commons eventually gave way again to commercial pressure.* Fortunately, nineteenth-century real estate developers were attuned to the fact that land adjacent to a park is more valuable than otherwise equivalent land. A number of them set aside small plazas and squares in their residential developments. Franklin Circle and Lincoln Park on Cleveland's West Side are surviving proof of their foresight.

With the emergence of manufacturing as a new sector of the Cleveland economy, public

---

*The concept of eliminating crosstown traffic from the Square—an excellent one—has resurfaced from time to time, most recently as a largely ignored proposal in a 1998 study of public-realm amenities spearheaded by the Committee on Public Art. Architectural historian Steven McQuillan has since taken up advocacy of this common-sensical idea. McQuillan estimates that it would cost roughly $10 million to make the upgrades needed to reroute traffic in a one-way pattern around the perimeter of Public Square. This is not a princely sum when compared to the aesthetic and recreational gains.

demand grew for places to escape noise and grime. In 1865 city council formed a subcommittee to study the problem but then declined to act on its findings, which called for the purchase of three parks comprising seventy-seven acres on the lakefront downtown, fifty acres on the East Side between Cedar and Kinsman avenues near Willson (East 55th Street), and seventy-five acres along Detroit Street on the near West Side. "The lake front [park] would increase the reputation of the city as a place of summer resort to such a degree as to make it a rival of Newport as a watering place," the subcommittee argued, with no success.

According to a 1910 history of Cleveland by Samuel P. Orth, only when a group of leading citizens made their feelings known in a private meeting with the mayor in 1867 did the parks proposal gain sufficient momentum to move through city council. That year council passed a resolution favoring the creation of a lakefront park.

Nothing further happened until 1871, when, acting on the authority of a new state law, council established Cleveland's first board of park commissioners. In 1873 the commissioners issued a parks bond to raise the funds to purchase a narrow strip of hillside between Erie (East 9th) and Seneca (West 3rd) Streets that overlooked the lake and intervening railroad tracks. After the removal of a shantytown and the addition of landscaped carriage drives and footpaths, this nine-acre plot became Lake View Park. The shift of residential populations away from downtown and an increase in rail traffic eventually brought about Lake View's demise, but a precedent for strong citizen support of public expenditures on parks had been set. This was to be the enduring foundation on which subsequent generations of parks proponents built.

The city of Cleveland's greatest era of park creation came in the 1890s, once again in response to public pressure. Influential citizens who believed that their community merited a comprehensive system of parks and boulevards commensurate with what they perceived to be its preeminence in culture, art, science, and industry held town meetings and lobbied the state legislature. An 1888 pamphlet entitled *Public Parks: A Compilation of Facts and Statistics* encapsulated their basic argument, which was that Cleveland "scarcely [made] a respectable showing" in terms of its parks holdings when compared with eleven other American cities ranging from New York to Cincinnati. Those communities boasted an average of one acre of parklands for every 484 citizens, while Clevelanders had to make do with one acre of green for every 2,200 citizens. Finally, in 1893 the state legislature was persuaded to pass legislation enabling Cleveland to establish a new and more powerful parks commission, of which the mayor and president of city council were ex officio members.

Through a combination of munificent gifts and astute purchases, the new parks commission succeeded in realizing the better part of its master plan, conceived by Boston landscape architect E. W. Bowditch. Seven great municipal parks were set aside, each located on the outskirts of Cleveland, some linked by parkways. This "band of verdure"—starting on the lakefront at Edgewater Park on the West Side and stretching along a parkway (West Boulevard) to Brookside Park, skipping east to Washington and Garfield Parks, hop-scotching back to the lakefront at Gordon Park, and extending through Rockefeller and Wade Parks and out the East Boulevard "parkway" toward Shaker Lakes Park—was denounced at the time of its creation by some as an amenity for the rich.

True enough, these outlying parks were most readily accessible to those with an independent means of transportation. Yet, like the emerging public school and library systems, they were also profoundly democratic in spirit: "a harmonious development of sylvan beauty to which all are welcome, rich and poor alike, where all may find rest and inspiration and pleasure," as the commissioners phrased it in an early report. The spread of electrified streetcar service eventually put these magnificent open spaces within easier reach of the general public. Sheltering "giant beeches, oaks and elms," to quote the commissioners' report again, "drooping willows shading pellucid pools; wide stretches of green lawn with banks of sweet-scented, vari-colored blossoms, tiny streams of crystal clear water running over beds of rock and sand; [and] larger streams flanking deep, cool recesses, where summer heat scarce finds itself able to penetrate," the municipal parks quickly insinuated themselves into the hearts of average Clevelanders.

It remained only for a few other visionaries to refine Clevelanders' conception of the ideal park. At the turn of the century, Conrad Mizer, a tailor and classical music lover, persuaded city officials to sponsor a season of summer band concerts in the parks. Mizer's brainchild became a staple of parks programming. Progressive mayor Tom L. Johnson (1901–9) encouraged the *active* use of parks by removing the "Keep Off the Grass" signs, building sports fields, ice-skating rinks, and children's playgrounds, and converting shelter houses to dance pavilions. Three decades later, the Work Projects Administration installed parking lots and modernized recreational facilities. By the 1930s, when thousands of Clevelanders took to the parks each night with their bedding, sleeping under the stars to escape the summer heat, the public's sense of ownership of the municipal parks clearly had been established.

As Cleveland evolved into a sprawling metropolis—by 1910 it was the country's sixth largest city, home to more than 560,000 residents—it became obvious that the common good required the preservation of "natural beauty spots" beyond the municipality's borders. Or so Cleveland's chief engineer of parks, William A. Stinchcomb, began to argue in 1905. Even before winning election as Cuyahoga County engineer in 1912, Stinchcomb helped write the 1911 legislation that enabled the establishment of county park boards in Ohio. In 1921 he became the first director of the Cleveland Metropolitan Park Board, which had been set up five years before. For the next fifty years Stinchcomb was "Mr. Metropolitan Park," overseeing every aspect of the development of one of the first and finest *metropolitan* park districts in America. No detail escaped his attention. He even succeeded in gilding the lily by calling for ring-necked pheasants to be released in the district's first two reservations.

While Bill Stinchcomb deserves lasting recognition as the mastermind of Cleveland's famed "Emerald Necklace," the fourteen-reservation chain of green could never have been assembled, equipped, and maintained without the active financial support of average citizens. The original enabling legislation had empowered county park boards to seek gifts of land. During the first five years of its existence, the Cleveland Metropolitan Park Board acquired about 1,000 acres via this mechanism. At that rate of growth, the nearly 20,000 acres of parklands that comprise today's Cleveland Metroparks could never have been assembled. Fortunately, Ohio parks law was amended in 1920 to give county park boards their animating force: the ability to issue bonds for land acquisition and to place operating levies on the ballot.

With the quality of life to be enjoyed by future generations of Greater Clevelanders hanging in the balance, the Cleveland Recreational Council, a coordinating body operating under the auspices of the Welfare Federation of Cleveland, stepped forward to push for the passage of a special tax levy that would allow the metropolitan park board to purchase property. The council led a contingent of fifty influential citizens on a fact-finding mission to Bear Mountain Park in New York State. The opinion leaders returned singing the praises of rural parks, and this groundswell of favorable talk helped to push the levy over the top in 1920. Once again, an important precedent had been set. Believing their tax dollars to be well invested, county taxpayers routinely pass Cleveland Metroparks operating levies and bond issues.

By contrast, the health of Cleveland's great municipal parks depended on allocations from the city's general revenue budget; there was no separate taxing authority to support their maintenance. Yet both county and city parks emerged from the Depression in better shape than ever. Work Projects Administration and Civilian Conservation Corps programs built needed recreational facilities in the still largely undeveloped Cleveland Metroparks and revitalized those in the city.

The infusion of federal resources postponed the day of reckoning for Cleveland city parks for a time. However, in the 1970s, funding for parks operations and maintenance began to diminish as a consequence of the gradual erosion of the city's tax base. With Cleveland's population and manufacturing strength on a slow decline, there seemed to be no stopping the deterioration of the great municipal parks—and of neighborhood parks and green spaces, as well. Signs of neglect—litter, boarded-up toilets and closed concessions, untended lawns, overgrown sports fields—gave credence to the growing impression that Cleveland's parks were unsafe. This perception had a dampening effect on both patronage and annual parks allocations, and so the spiral continued downward.

With the complete desecration of Gordon Park on Cleveland's East Side, bottom was hit. The park's core parcel of 122 acres had been bequeathed to the citizens of Cleveland by William J. Gordon in 1892. Even before the land was transferred to the city, Gordon Park was beloved by Clevelanders. Some ten years previously, Gordon (the head of the largest wholesale grocery house west of the Alleghenies, a real estate developer, and a pioneer importer of iron ore for manufacturing purposes) had opened the grounds of his lakefront estate to the public. He wanted his fellow citizens to enjoy his handiwork: the miles of graveled carriage paths, the rustic bridges, the stone stairways leading down to natural grottos, the exquisite landscaping of the Ramble, the Evergreen Lawn and other evocatively named sections of the estate, the boathouse, the miniature lighthouse, the little chapel erected in the memory of his late daughter. In leaving this wonderland to the city, Gordon had asked only that it be kept open forever to the public and that nothing ever be done to block the park's lake view.

For some sixty years these provisions helped to protect Gordon Park from the kind of industrial and commercial developments that had despoiled other sections of Cleveland's lakeshore. By the early 1950s, however, commuters, truckers, and business interests were pressing for improvements to the county's inadequate system of roads. Planners eager to facilitate the flow of traffic from the far eastern edges of the metropolitan area into downtown Cleveland ignored the presence of Gordon Park in laying out the route of a proposed new freeway that would connect with the Memorial Shoreway. The construction of Interstate 90 ripped the park in two.

Adding insult to this grievous injury to the physical integrity and serenity of the park, the Cleveland service department subsequently decided to create a landfill in the park's northeast quadrant. Into it went junked cars and refuse. Although the landfill was intended ultimately to become a recreational area, its immediate effect was to attract others who wished also to be rid of their trash, construction debris, and discarded appliances. With parks maintenance crews and security officers stretched thin, illegal dumping became epidemic at the landfill.

In the fall of 1971 the unsightly mess spontaneously ignited. Firefighters were unable to extinguish the blaze completely, and it smoldered until the following spring. In the intervening months the smoke-filled air at Gordon Park served as a potent symbol of the pall that hung over most of the city's parks and playgrounds. The Growth Association of Greater Cleveland, a chamber of commerce, attempted to counter the bad image by sponsoring the first Parties in the Park in 1973. Luring crowds back to the parks with free music, these Friday-night gatherings proved to be a popular summer tradition for more than fifteen years. They were an important early step toward the rehabilitation of the city's parks because they conveyed the essential value of public open space: as a physical venue within which to meet interesting people and have fun.

Elsewhere in the region, the fresh breeze of environmental activism was quickening. Even before concern over the pollution of America's air and water and the loss of natural habitats to development coalesced into a national movement on the first Earth Day in April 1970, the issue of environmental quality had struck a responsive chord in Greater Clevelanders. In addition to losing the full enjoyment of Cleveland's parks, they found themselves confronted with a dying lake, a burning river, and the threatened disappearance of the region's largest and most beautiful open space: the Cuyahoga River Valley. From this ferment there emerged throughout northeast Ohio individual activists, ad hoc groups, community development corporations, and not-for-profit organizations that believed, in the spirit of the 1960s and '70s, that they could make a difference in the quality of the local environment. Working in diverse settings throughout the region, environmental champions of all stripes would usher in (among other conservation initiatives) a new era of parks advocacy.

In the early days of the emerging parks movement, citizen opposition to insensitive urban planning resulted in signal victories. Cuyahoga County's attempt to construct Interstate 290 was stopped cold in the mid-1960s because it imperiled the Shaker Lakes parklands through which Doan Brook runs. Born of this protest, the Nature Center at Shaker Lakes now serves as a leading protector and interpreter of the Doan Brook watershed. A campaign to save Mentor Marsh was launched in the early '60s; its initial objective was to prevent Lake County from dredging the marsh so that it could be used by recreational boaters. Gaining force, the conservation campaign culminated in 1971 in the creation of one of the first state nature preserves, ensuring the long-term survival of this irreplaceable wetlands.

Sometimes the catalyst for citizen action was official indifference. In 1977, for example, a grass-roots coalition formed a new not-for-profit agency called Rapid Recovery to assume responsibility for cleaning up and enhancing the appearance of Cleveland's rapid-transit corridor. The agency's founders were embarrassed that the litter-strewn landscape through which the city's Rapid line passed was the first sight visitors to Cleveland encountered. In the 1980s Rapid Recovery branched out under the banner of Clean-Land, Ohio, asking area corporations to underwrite and maintain several dozen "City Side Gardens" on major thoroughfares. To commemorate Cleveland's bicentennial in 1996, Clean-Land raised the monies to plant 10,000 shade trees in neighborhood parks and schoolyards, and, under contract with Cleveland Public Power, planted an additional 40,000 shade trees on tree lawns and at prominent intersections throughout the city.

By the end of the century Clean-Land had evolved into ParkWorks. The new not-for-profit parks advocacy organization began to work with the city of Cleveland to raise funds for needed capital improvements in the parks and to supplement their recreational programming. ParkWorks also teamed with the Cleveland Municipal School District and City Hall to plan and build public school playgrounds.

The lesson was clear. When individual and institutional parks advocates joined forces with government officials and the private sector, they could accomplish things that no single entity could manage alone. As the twenty-first century dawned, the combined efforts of dozens of public-private partnerships—each built around mutual recognition that parks and green spaces add economic, social, civic, environmental, and aesthetic value to cities and neighborhoods—had produced an impressive record of achievement. Parks proponents had established six new parks along the upper Cuyahoga River and saved Eastman Reading Garden, a rare pocket of green in downtown Cleveland, from the bulldozer. They had enhanced public access to Cleveland's lakefront through the creation of North Coast Harbor and Voinovich Park. And they had reclaimed neglected green spaces in residential areas throughout the city, including a neighborhood commons in Tremont (Lincoln Park), a community park in Glenville (Forest Hills), and a major municipal park (Rockefeller) adjoining University Circle.

Cleveland Metroparks had added two new reservations in the center of Cuyahoga County to better serve the needs of inner-city residents. The city of Mentor had set aside Mentor Lagoons as a nature preserve to protect its pristine beach and upland forest habitats, and Mill Creek waterfall (Cuyahoga County's tallest) had found champions intent on showcasing this natural attraction as part of a neighborhood redevelopment strategy. Yet there was no more important conservation triumph than the establishment of 33,000-acre Cuyahoga Valley National Park (formerly the Cuyahoga Valley National Recreation Area) between Akron and Cleveland.

To reiterate: These park-building efforts, some of which are described in greater detail in the following pages, have one common element. None could have succeeded without public-private teamwork and resources. Yet it is important also to note that behind every great park there usually stands a single individual, a person who had the vision, the tenacity, and the leadership skills needed to rally other supporters to the park's cause.

The story of the decline of Cleveland's lakefront parks has a happy ending because of one of the many grass-roots visionaries credited in this book—landscape architect William A. Behnke. Watching the growing trash heap in Gordon Park, Behnke became incensed and decided that he was not going to keep silent anymore. He began speaking out about the park's abuse to every community group willing to listen, and his protest set off a chain of actions that eventually resulted in the transfer of management responsibility for Edgewater, Gordon, and Wildwood Parks to the Ohio Department of Natural Resources.

The Towpath Trail. Now more than twenty miles long, the bike and hike path will stretch from downtown Cleveland into central Ohio. With thirty neighborhood spurs and connectors already planned, the trail's potential to spark the "re-greening" of Greater Cleveland is immense.

Similarly, Ralph Regula, a young state senator from Navarre, Ohio, took it upon himself to prevent the Ohio & Erie Canal from being sold off piecemeal by the state in the 1960s. Regula, who had enjoyed hiking along the canal towpath as a boy, persuaded the Stark County Commissioners to take title to the canal lands in their jurisdiction, setting an example of stewardship that would be emulated by other authorities throughout northeast Ohio.

After the Cuyahoga Valley National Park was created in 1974, ensuring the protection of another stretch of the canal, citizen-stewards in Cleveland and Akron took up the quest to preserve sections located to the north and south of CVNP's boundaries. Working independently at first, their advocacy groups—the North Cuyahoga Valley Corridor and the Ohio & Erie Canal Coalition—teamed with the local and national officials of the National Park

Service to prepare a unified plan for the protection and development of the canal corridor. Released in 1993, *A Route to Prosperity* served as the impetus for seeking official recognition of the canal's historic significance.

Clearly, there would be no Ohio & Erie Canal National Heritage Corridor today had not Ralph Regula first acted to keep intact the canal, a unique example of nineteenth-century transportation technology. Yet little else might have transpired had hiker Jeff Lennartz and historic preservationist Tom Yablonsky not also been willing to act on their love of the canal. They formed the North Cuyahoga Valley Corridor (NCVC), which, in partnership with the Cuyahoga County Planning Commission, made the first serious effort to articulate a vision of an interconnected canal corridor.

Still, the concept that has come to be known popularly as CanalWay Ohio might have died aborning had not still other visionary and resourceful individuals, such as Timothy Donovan, director of Ohio Canal Corridor (formerly NCVC); Dan Rice, director of the Ohio & Erie Canal Coalition; and John Debo, superintendent of the Cuyahoga Valley National Park, stepped forward to flesh it out. Tireless advocates, this trio of leaders helped to build a broad base of support for the establishment of a National Heritage Corridor (NHC) among the region's powers-that-be. In 1996 the four-county coalition of CanalWay proponents won NHC designation from Congress.

At present, CanalWay may be best known as the catalyst for the construction of the Towpath Trail, an all-weather path (enjoyed by 1.7 million hikers and bikers annually) that parks proponents hope will one day stretch from Cleveland's Flats to New Philadephia in the heart of Tuscarawas County. However, the completion of the Towpath Trail is likely to mark only the beginning, not the end, of CanalWay's development. If past is prologue, citizen-leaders throughout northeast Ohio will move to ensure that their communities take maximum advantage of this green version of an "Empowerment Zone" to enhance their recreational resources. Greater Cleveland's golden era of parks may well lie ahead.

LINCOLN PARK

The People's Commons

CLEVELAND'S TREMONT NEIGHBORHOOD

Something unexpected occurred at the 1999 Tremont Arts & Cultural Festival in Lincoln Park, a grassy commons occupying a rectangular city block between West 11th and 14th Streets and Kenilworth and Starkweather Avenues on Cleveland's near South Side. A four-year-old girl got lost. She had been playing on the swing sets in the festival's "children's village," where Cleveland Metroparks Zoo was displaying barn owls and boa constrictors, and where kids could have their faces painted and exchange violent toys for books. At some point little Eva disappeared from her mother's sight into the throng of people who had gathered in one of Cleveland's oldest parks on a Saturday afternoon to celebrate the cultural vitality of Tremont, a South Side neighborhood situated on the bluffs of the Cuyahoga River.

Panicked, the mother ran over to the festival's "performing village," which was offering a day-long lineup of entertainment (beginning with bagpipe music by Kevin Kelly and ending with acid jazz by Rhesus Amok). A public-address station had been set up nearby in the contemporary gazebo in the middle of the park. Tremont councilman Joe Cimperman stood at the mike, offering his thanks to the festival organizers: Merrick House neighborhood center, the Tremont Arts Organization, and Tremont West Development Corporation. When the frantic woman reached his side and began yelling about her missing daughter, Cimperman

Tremont Arts and Cultural Festival at Lincoln Park. Having a common meeting ground helps to build a sense of community in one of Cleveland's most ethnically, racially, and socially diverse neighborhoods.

broke off his comments. Upon learning what had transpired, the Ward 13 councilman turned back to the mike and announced: "We have a little four-year-old girl who's lost."

What happened next was hard to believe, but it said something about how a park can help to alleviate the anonymity and isolation of urban life and build a sense of community, even in a neighborhood as ethnically, racially, and socially mixed as Tremont. (Since the 1860s, when the city's first steel mills began operation, Tremont had been home to successive waves of immigrants from many lands, all attracted to the neighborhood by the nearness of jobs in the industrial valley below.) A hush fell over the crowd of blacks, whites, and Latinos, and everyone froze in place—church ladies and punks, stilt walkers and mimes, people in wheelchairs and parents pushing strollers, activists handing out leaflets and senior citizens selling Eastern European crafts, young lovers and bikers, Irish balladeers and Mexican ballet dancers, cellular phone vendors and amateur artisans—all momentarily united in their dismay and concern. The silence—palpable as the smell of frying tortillas in the air—lasted for many seconds.

Cimperman came back on mike to explain where the child had last been seen. Several people rushed off with the mother in that direction to search for her, and within a few moments the little girl had been located. "Welcome back, little Eva," Cimperman cooed over the PA system. "We love you, future citizen of Cleveland, future voter."

Olmsted's Law. Public parks are "the only places" where "vast numbers of persons [are] brought closely together, poor and rich, young and old . . . each individual adding by his mere presence to the pleasure of all others."

The tableau vivant in the park began to break apart, as the crowd turned back to the business of promenading and people-watching.

Lincoln Park made an ideal venue for both activities. The parade of humanity streaming through the commons was more diverse, more fiercely individualistic, than one would typically see in a single spot in Greater Cleveland. For onlookers of a certain age the lively scene evoked memories of "happenings" in the 1960s. Those of a more scholarly bent may have been reminded of the democratic impulses that launched the parks movement in this country in the 1860s.

Studded with magnificent sycamores, under whose spreading branches a network of paths invitingly wind, surrounded on all four sides by an interesting mélange of historic and newly renovated homes, storefronts, and churches, Lincoln Park is a simple but elegantly proportioned "pleasure ground."* The prominence of its location hints at the neighborhood's long-ago aspiration to become a gracious college town. The land was first reserved for use as a commons by one Thirsa Pelton, who intended to establish a women's college on the surrounding sixty-nine-acre parcel she had purchased in 1850. Thus tiny Lincoln Park is a virtual contemporary of New York City's Central Park, the archetypal pleasure ground.

---

*This description, applied to America's first parks, reflects their function as pastoral escapes from the unaesthetic city.

Central Park was designed in 1858 by landscape architect and pioneering city planner Frederick Law Olmsted, who took his aesthetic cues from the private gardens and preserves enjoyed by European nobility. But his objectives had an egalitarian twist. As Olmsted saw it, public parks should be more than desperately needed retreats from the dirt, noise, and congestion of life in nineteenth-century America's burgeoning industrial centers. Olmsted believed parks could be a tool for uplifting the toiling classes. Provide the immigrants who were flooding into urban sweatshops and slums with free and convenient access to a pastoral setting in which they could sedately spend their leisure—exposed to clean air, their social betters, and the beauty of nature—and over time the experience would improve their health, manners, and moral character, he believed. In truly functioning as Olmsted intended—as common ground where individuals of all social and ethnic backgrounds feel comfortable mixing, as indeed "the only places," as Olmsted saw it, where "vast numbers of persons [are] brought closely together, poor and rich, young and old . . . each individual adding by his mere presence to the pleasure of all others"—Lincoln Park and Central Park are sisters in spirit, as well as contemporaries.

The overnight success of Central Park inspired a host of new commissions for Olmsted's firm throughout the country, as big-city governments responded to growing pressure to provide healthful recreation with a rush of park building. Olmsted went astray, however, in insisting that his "pleasure grounds" be used exclusively for activities that he considered decorous. Strolling, ice skating, and boating were allowed in Central Park; oratory, military marches, and rowdy behavior were not.

Like their counterparts in New York City, the South Siders who picnicked and hunted squirrels in Pelton's Private Park (as Lincoln Park was originally called) refused to be dictated to. After Pelton died in 1853, her heirs installed a fence around the property and locked the gates. Time and again the fence was torn down by frustrated park users who lived in what was then known as University Heights. (Although Pelton never realized her dream of founding a college for women, a group of prominent citizens led by Cleveland mayor Samuel Starkweather *had* succeeded in establishing a university in the neighborhood. The doors of Cleveland University remained open only from 1850 to 1855, but the distinctive names of such present-day Tremont streets as Literary and Professor attest to its brief existence.)

Bitter litigation upheld the rights of Pelton's heirs to exclude the public from the

Always a popular refuge. Lincoln Park was originally set aside in the 1850s as the commons for a private women's college, but neighbors kept tearing down fences erected to keep the public out.

commons, but eventually the owners realized theirs was a lost cause. The people would have their park, no matter what the courts ruled. In 1879 Cleveland's parks commission was finally able to acquire the land from the heirs for $50,000. On the Fourth of July in 1880, according to a Cleveland *Plain Dealer* newspaper article, "the entire South Side celebrated the final opening of the park with a grand barbecue."

On the occasion of Cleveland's centennial in 1896, the commons was outfitted with a fountain and an ornate bandstand. It was then renamed Lincoln Square Park, an appellation that came from the park's use during the Civil War as a parade ground by Union Army encampments, a few of whose red-brick military buildings can still be seen in Tremont. In the early years of the twentieth century a public bathhouse opened on the park's south end, and Merrick settlement house began operations in two storefronts at the southeast corner of the park, having chosen this particular location to enable the children it served to take advantage of the playground that had been built in Lincoln Park with funds donated by a supportive local brewer. Otherwise little changed in the commons during its first hundred years, except for the ethnicity of the people who patronized it.

The Irish and Germans were the first immigrants to settle in the area in the 1860s. They were succeeded by Polish laborers in the 1890s. The Poles moved on at the turn of the cen-

Up from the bottom. The pool has not always been a source of delight. During the 1970s, when park maintenance declined, vandals threw bottles, sofas, and even a car into the water.

tury, to be replaced by Greeks and Syrians. Displaced Ukrainians followed in the 1950s. Each new generation of residents regarded Lincoln Park as a prized community asset, and it remained a centerpiece of life in Tremont through World War II and beyond.

During the Depression, the bandstand, once the site of monthly concerts, became a distribution point for free milk. Kids who grew up in the neighborhood in the 1940s, like Jim Noga, owner of Noga Floral Shop on West 14th, remember the park's beautiful flower garden, the ever-present cop on the beat, and carefree summer days spent wading in the fountain or playing baseball on one of three diamonds. Tremont mothers felt safe allowing their children to return to the park grounds after dinner, to build bonfires, tell stories, and roast potatoes. In the 1950s the decrepit Victorian-era bandstand finally had to be torn down, but a swimming pool was built near the spot where this popular landmark had stood. Now the pool became Lincoln Park's chief attraction.

By the 1970s some of the attention the pool attracted began to be troubling. The construction of Interstate 71 through the middle of Tremont in the mid-1960s dislocated hundreds of families and tore a hole in the social fabric of the neighborhood. Housing values declined. Newcomers tended to be less affluent and, with Cleveland itself sliding toward default, there were fewer and fewer resources available to maintain Lincoln Park. Its unkempt appearance bred acts of disrespect. Frequently mothers bringing their kids to the Learn to

Riding to the rescue. Lincoln Park's downward spiral was halted by a single determined individual, who organized a volunteer cleanup effort in the late 1970s that inspired others to get involved in the restoration of the commons.

Swim program discovered that the morning session had been canceled. The lifeguards were busy cleaning up broken glass left behind by after-hours drinkers, who had tossed their empty beer bottles onto the deck of the pool. On other occasions lifeguards arriving for work found sofas and even a car submerged in the water. After thieves broke into the park's comfort station and stole the copper plumbing, swimmers went showerless because the city parks department lacked replacement parts.

In the 1970s a single individual took it upon herself to try to end this downward spiral of neglect and abuse. After cutting her shoe on a piece of glass while walking through the commons in 1978, Kenilworth Avenue resident Charlene Dina organized a volunteer trash cleanup with the help of Nick Gentile, director of the Lincoln Recreation Center headquartered in the old public bathhouse. This marked the beginning of the park's comeback. The following year, Tremont West Development Corporation (TWDC) was organized, and its staff was to assume responsibility for working with the city to keep the park clean and its facilities in good repair. The park also became a cause for Tremont's newest residents: artists, young professionals, shop owners and restaurateurs attracted by the affordability and charm of the century architecture. Led by these urban pioneers, the community pulled together in the late 1980s to raise $25,000 for a new gazebo for the park. It was erected by volunteers in a single day.

Stabilizing influence. The park's rebirth has contributed to Tremont's success in attracting new residents and market-rate housing.

Through the efforts of concerned Tremont residents, Lincoln Park has reclaimed its place of distinction as "the people's park." Today joggers do laps around its perimeter (four laps to a mile); senior citizens occupy its benches. Touch football games are a fall tradition. At Eastertide there are church processions around the park's perimeter. The homeless men served by neighboring St. Augustine's come over regularly to pick up the trash, and each December the gazebo is decorated for the holidays by TWDC, the park's unofficial watchdog.

TWDC director Emily Lipovan Holan calls Lincoln Park a "jewel." It has certainly been a factor in the success of TWDC's joint ventures with private developers, which have resulted in the construction of new single-family homes in Tremont and the conversion of the former Lincoln Park Bathhouse into upscale condominiums. Eager to enhance the park's "stabilizing influence" on the neighborhood, TWDC plants spring bulbs, worries over the health of its irreplaceable trees, and plans to make the Art & Cultural Festival an annual event.

In truth, the people of Tremont no longer really need the excuse of formal programming to make themselves at home in Lincoln Park. Their shared stewardship of this historic green has given them something the interstate highway temporarily took away: a sense of neighborliness. Tremont's example suggests a way that other urban neighborhoods might begin to heal their social fractures and build a common identity: rally around a community park.

FINE ARTS GARDEN

A Place to Remember

UNIVERSITY CIRCLE, CLEVELAND

The Fine Arts Garden truly deserves its designation as the "front door" of Cleveland's University Circle. Created during the mid-1920s, it reflects the educated tastes of the city's industrial leaders, who went to great lengths to ensure that the Cleveland Museum of Art, the repository of treasures from the collections of prominent Clevelanders, was enshrined in an appropriately elegant setting. Indeed, the jewel-like, five-acre park is perhaps the most outstanding example of commemorative landscape architecture in northeast Ohio.

The Old World stonework, idyllic landscaping, and allegorical statuary in the Fine Arts Garden enchant people from all walks of life. Of all the plazas, squares, and green spaces in the region that are home to monuments and memorials, only the Cleveland Cultural Gardens in nearby Rockefeller Park rivals the garden's beauty as a milieu for public art.

Despite the Fine Arts Garden's preeminence, some Clevelanders may not be aware of its official name. The bridal parties who use it as a romantic backdrop for wedding pictures, the students from Cleveland Institute of Art who amble over to sketch the sculpture, the toddlers brought by their parents or day-care guardians to admire the lagoon, and the workers from all over the Circle who power-walk there during their lunch hours—all these folks probably refer to the spot as "Wade Lagoon." The nickname derives from the garden's most prominent feature, a lovely, if manufactured, pond.

Wade's legacy. In 1882 Western Union Company co-founder Jeptha H. Wade donated land on the outskirts of Cleveland to create the city's first large public park. An ornamental lake, still known as Wade Lagoon, is one of the park's few surviving features.

The pond was one of many improvements made by the city to the public park in which the Museum of Art is located. Bounded by Doan Brook, a seventy-five-acre parcel of land at the eastern end of Euclid Avenue was donated to the people of Cleveland in 1882 by Western Union Telegraph Company co-founder Jeptha H. Wade. At the time, skeptics suggested that the wealthy businessman was only attempting to increase the value of the new homes he planned to build and sell in the surrounding Wade Allotment, but members of the public cared nothing about the details of how they had finally gained access to what had formerly been known as Euclid Avenue Park. The previous owner had strictly limited admission to the carriage drives that wound through the idyllic property.

"Its magnificent grove of forest trees, the picturesque valley of Doan brook and the stretches of open land," a 1910 history of Cleveland notes, "made [Wade] park a popular resort from the first." With the addition of a boathouse, a band shell, and an octagonal animal house where "two black bears, two catamounts, or wild cats, a family of crows, a pair of foxes and a colony of prairie dogs" were the first exhibits, Wade Park became a runaway success. On weekends and holidays it was thronged by thousands of adults and children. The zoo was transferred to Brookside Park in 1907 to permit its further development, but

A perfect setting. Shocked that the grounds of the Cleveland Museum of Art had yet to be landscaped ten years after the museum was built in Wade Park, the members of the Garden Club of Cleveland took it upon themselves to see that the handsome neoclassical building was appropriately enshrined.

for more than forty years Clevelanders enjoyed boating on the lagoon. The memory of that delightful pastime has apparently been imprinted on the civic consciousness, even though, during the installation of the Fine Arts Garden, the sixteen-foot-tall centaur fountain that splashed in the center of the lagoon was removed and the Depression put an end to the boating concession. The pond now served another important purpose: as a reflecting pool for the museum's handsome neoclassical façade.

Today many Clevelanders know the Fine Arts Garden only as this picture-postcard view, glimpsed from the car window during the daily commute. (Similarly, those who are familiar with the Cultural Gardens only from the vantage point of Martin Luther King, Jr., Boulevard, Rockefeller Park's main drive, may be tempted to dismiss them as simply stonework.)

University Circle's front door. The Old World stonework, idyllic landscaping, and allegorical statuary in the Fine Arts Garden make a positive first impression on visitors to one of the world's premier cultural meccas.

So masterful is the landscape architecture of the Fine Arts Garden, that some may take its perfection completely for granted, as if the garden had been there from time immemorial. The magician responsible for this illusion was Frederick Law Olmsted, Jr., of Brookline, Massachusetts, son of the legendary landscape architect.

The artwork commissioned to adorn the garden also gives the appearance of being inevitably right—but only to those who have not read the correspondence between Olmsted *fils* and New York sculptor Chester Beach. Beach created the monumental, Roman-influenced *Fountain of the Waters* that is the centerpiece of the Nature Court, an oval formal garden that occupies the space between the museum and the lagoon. The two men went back and forth about the size and height of the white Georgian marble fountain, trying to determine the proper proportions of the upper bowl and the lower basin. They were debating a difference of inches.

Beach also designed the variegated-green marble statuary representing the twelve signs of the Zodiac placed in niches in the hedge encircling the Nature Court, as well as the fountain's companion bronzes: the kneeling female *Earth,* who gathers to her the water from the rivers of the world with her right hand, and the male *Sun,* an archer whose arrow sends the waters into the clouds. Visible from the south steps of the museum, this suite of sculpture is the most prominent of the garden's artistic riches. All told, there are thirty pieces of

Earth. This companion piece to the garden's monumental fountain (both by sculptor Chester Beach) is one of thirty sculptures in the immediate vicinity of the art museum.

sculpture on display in the garden and in several adjoining green spaces. To fully appreciate this treasury of public art, one must explore the area on foot.

Parks have from the *beginning* served commemorative purposes. Even before the Fine Arts Garden was created, Clevelanders regarded Wade Park, the city's first large public park, as an especially fitting location for a number of monumental bronze statues honoring leaders they admired. *Louis Kossuth,* a statue of the Hungarian national hero who led his country's struggle for independence from Austria (and came to Cleveland in 1852 to raise funds for Hungarian relief work), was erected by the Magyar American Citizens of Cleveland on Euclid Avenue near Stearns Road in 1902. Two years later *Tadeusz Kosciuszko,* a statue of the Polish national who fought for American independence in the Revolutionary War, went up on a rise in what is now the garden area west of the museum. (Cleveland's Polish community is discussing the possibility of repatriating the statue by moving it to a prominent location in Slavic Village.) And at the intersection of MLK Boulevard and Jeptha Drive, Slovakian general Milan Stefanik is commemorated in bronze.

From an artistic point of view, the most important of Wade Park's monuments is Augustus Saint-Gaudens's *Marcus Alonzo Hanna,* which portrays the Cleveland industrialist credited with masterminding William McKinley's election to the presidency in 1896. Located at

Marcus Alonzo Hanna *by Augustus Saint-Gaudens.* Even before the Fine Arts Garden was created, Clevelanders regarded Wade Park as an especially fitting location for monumental bronzes commemorating revered leaders.

the intersection of Euclid and Chester Avenues, the monument, which dates from 1907, is the only outdoor sculpture by the famous French artist in the state of Ohio. However, don't overlook the statue by Cleveland artist James G. C. Hamilton that stands on the east side of the museum. This heroic 1899 bronze is a tribute to Harvey Rice, a Cleveland schoolteacher who went on, as a state senator, to secure passage in 1853 of legislation creating a system of common schools in Ohio. Hamilton also created the Moses Cleaveland sculpture on Public Square.

Of the art commissioned or chosen specially to enhance the Fine Arts Garden, perhaps the most interesting is *Night Passing the Earth to Day,* a bronze sculpture of two female figures supporting a large globe, the surface of which is a sundial. This allegorical piece, which stands at the foot of the Holden terrace at the Euclid Avenue end of the garden, is by Frank Luis Jirouch, a popular Cleveland sculptor of Czech extraction. It is as a working timepiece that the *Night/Day* truly amazes. Created in 1928, the piece incorporated what was said at the time to be the only successful curved-surface sundial in the world.

Jirouch also conceived the garden's most delightful sculpture, *Spring Racing the Wind,* a 1929 bronze of a young draped woman, her hair and cape tossed back as she runs with flowers in her hand and birds frolicking in a pond at her feet. Originally commissioned as a lawn adornment for a Cleveland estate, the piece can be found to the northeast of the lagoon. It was donated to the garden by a member of the Garden Club of Cleveland.

Fine Arts Garden

Spring Racing the Wind. Every art-work in the garden has recently been cleaned as part of a conservation program spearheaded by The Sculpture Center of Cleveland. Frank Luis Jirouch's 1929 bronze now looks as pristine as on the day it was created to decorate the lawn of an area estate.

This elite social club was to make an immense contribution to the "greening" of the city. Not only did its members go on to found the Garden Center of Greater Cleveland (now Cleveland Botanical Garden), it was they who commissioned the Fine Arts Garden as a gift to the community.

Modern-day Clevelanders may find it impossible to believe that, nearly a decade after the Art Museum's construction, the parklands in front of the building had yet to be reland-scaped. The grounds had not even been reseeded. (Perhaps the inattention was a blessing in disguise; in 1923, city maintenance crews had swept through Wade Park, sprucing up the row-boats at the lagoon, a pergola behind the museum, and even an old war cannon that was on display with a fresh coat of paint. Unfortunately, to advertise that the work had been done, they chose the colors orange and black.) The unkempt appearance of the weedy, rubbish-strewn expanse in front of the museum was also distressing, especially to the members of the Garden Club of Cleveland.

These strong-willed and energetic society women took it upon themselves to do some-thing about the problem. Upon the establishment of a city manager plan in Cleveland in 1924, they invited the new city manager, officials from the city parks department, museum trustees, and other influential citizens to a meeting held in an upper room of Wade Park

A Place to Remember

Manor. The luxury residential hotel had been chosen as a gathering site because it afforded an excellent view of "the *shocking* lands lying between Euclid Avenue and the Museum of Art," as Eleanor Squire, one of the club members in attendance, later described the scene. Winning agreement from the powers-that-be that action must finally be taken, the Garden Club mounted an "Italian Street Fair" in 1925 to raise monies needed to begin planning for the site's beautification.

The cost of creating the Fine Arts Garden was about $500,000. The city absorbed the expense of culverting the section of Doan Brook that passed by the museum and on through University Circle. (The cosmetic surgery had been recommended by Olmsted, who sniffed that "the stiff old channel" added nothing to the charm of the area.) Private donations covered the remaining costs. Some of Cleveland's most prominent families sponsored each distinctive part of the garden. For example, Delia Holden (Mrs. Windsor T.) White underwrote the construction of the marble terrace and stairway leading down from Euclid Avenue. Sentimental reasons dictated her choice. In an earlier era that particular location had been part of the Holden family "farm."

No one was more committed to the Fine Arts Garden than Frances Sherwin, who was president of the Garden Club of Cleveland at the time the garden was conceived. Frances and her husband, John, underwrote the cost of constructing a marble terrace next to the museum and a marble staircase leading down to the Nature Court. The Sherwins later set up a $250,000 endowment to ensure the garden's proper upkeep. Mrs. Sherwin even went to the trouble of sending four swans into the city each summer from her Waite Hill farm to serve as grace notes for the lagoon.

Credit for the Fine Arts Garden, as well as for the Cleveland Cultural Gardens, must also be given to Cleveland city manager William R. Hopkins. A man of intellect and discernment, Hopkins recognized that both projects would promote intercultural exchange and goodwill—welcome salve for the wounds of hatred suffered by some ethnic groups in Cleveland during World War I. Each sculpture park received the city's fullest cooperation and financial support. Hopkins even helped to resolve a debate between Olmsted and the director of the Art Museum, who found themselves politely disagreeing over the issue of widening Wade lagoon. Each questioned the other's judgment about how wide the lagoon needed to be in order to fulfill its intended new function as a reflecting pool. The city man-

Return to greatness. A new master landscaping plan underwritten by the Fine Arts Garden Commission will reestablish the spirit of the original design by Olmsted Brothers. The sculptures demarcate the "Nature Court," the setting for the garden's *Fountain of the Waters.*

ager offered to construct a temporary enlargement of the basin to allow firsthand examination of the adequacy of the reflection.

Hopkins was a featured speaker at the garden dedication on July 23, 1928. The ceremony opened with a fanfare of trumpets and a procession. While the Cleveland Orchestra played Meyerbeer's "Coronation March," a double file of twenty-eight debutantes descended the front steps of the museum, carrying a festive daisy chain.

Inevitably, the Fine Arts Garden lost a measure of its opening-day freshness. Subsequent plantings strayed from the original design, and the sculptures began to show the ill effects of weather, pollution, vandalism, and neglect. The aging process has now been halted as a result of two separate but complementary initiatives. The first is "a testimony to a continuing tradition of public-spirited generosity on the part of private citizens of Cleveland," says Ruth S. Eppig, chairman of the Fine Arts Garden Commission, which administers the endowment established by the Sherwins. She is referring to an art restoration program that underwrote the professional cleaning of every piece of sculpture in or near the garden. Now each looks as pristine as the day it was carved or cast.

The restoration project was an initiative of the Outdoor Sculpture Conservation & Education Program of The Sculpture Center of Cleveland, a not-for-profit organization located in University Circle that fosters the careers of emerging sculptors through exhibitions of their work. In 1996, as its bicentennial gift to the city, The Sculpture Center began to raise funds from individuals, foundations, corporations, and organizations sympathetic to its other interest: promoting the preservation of outdoor sculpture throughout Ohio. The center concentrated first on cleaning important individual statues, such as those of Moses Cleaveland and Tom L. Johnson on Public Square and that of Abraham Lincoln on the Mall next to the Board of Education Building. In 1999, the Sculpture Center's former and new partners stepped forward to support the more ambitious conservation effort in the Fine Arts Garden, which was coordinated by staff member Juilee Decker. This initiative was subsequently designated by the National Trust for Historic Preservation as an official project of the Save America's Treasures Program.

Work is also underway to reestablish the spirit of Olmsted's original landscaping plan through selective replanting and removal of inappropriate plants that have been added over the years. To restore the crowd-pleasing spectacle of the garden awash in the colors of a profusion of flowering trees and bulbs each spring is one of the primary goals of the new master landscaping plan, prepared by Cleveland landscape architecture firm Behnke Associates at the behest of the Fine Arts Garden Commission. There is even talk among those envisioning the future of University Circle of possibly releasing Doan Brook from its concrete tomb. Imagine: a natural stream running once again through Wade Park.

An inscription found in the British Garden in Rockefeller Park captures the charms awaiting discovery in Cleveland's two outstanding sculpture parks. A quote from Shakespeare's *As You Like It,* the inscription reads:

> *Books in Running Brooks,*
> *Sermons in Stones,*
> *And Good in Everything.*

OHIO & ERIE CANAL RESERVATION

Observing Nature at Work

CUYAHOGA HEIGHTS

Catching a glimpse of a rare species is a thrill most people never experience outside a zoo. Yet that may be one of the many surprises awaiting visitors to the Ohio & Erie Canal Reservation, the newest Cleveland Metroparks unit.

The most distinctly urban of the fourteen parks in Cuyahoga County's famed "Emerald Necklace," the Ohio & Erie Canal Reservation opened in August 1999 on 325 acres of bottom land once intended for industrial use in the Cuyahoga River Valley. The park can be entered from East 49th Street in Cuyahoga Heights near a Birmingham Steel Company mill on Grant Avenue. At various other points in the Ohio & Erie Canal Reservation, an Illuminating Company/FirstEnergy Company substation, a BP Amoco petroleum-tank storage terminal, and a Northeast Ohio Regional Sewer District wastewater treatment plant adjoin its grounds. Forty-four trains a day rumble through the middle of the reservation on a 130-foot-high railroad trestle that dates from the early 1900s and stretches for 1,900 feet almost directly above the reservation's new nature center. The busy streets of Cuyahoga Heights and Valley View cut through the southernmost flanks of the reservation.

Strange though it may seem, all of this infrastructure—the life support systems of a big city—adds to the appeal and beauty of the park. The new reservation is also blessed with

Uncommon beauty. The urban infrastructure that surrounds and even penetrates the newest reservation in the Cleveland Metroparks system only adds to its appeal.

the presence of the meandering Cuyahoga River and the northernmost four miles of the Ohio & Erie Canal that still contain water. These two transportation routes fueled Cleveland's growth in the late eighteenth and early nineteenth centuries. The Ohio & Erie Canal Reservation has taken maximum advantage of this fascinating convergence of technology from three different centuries. In its new Leonard Krieger CanalWay Center the park offers an array of educational exhibits and programming on three themes: "Systems at Work," "People at Work," and "Nature at Work." The displays help visitors appreciate the broad sweep of regional economic history represented within the reservation boundaries.

Just as the park's untraditional setting causes astonishment, so do the lessons this gritty industrial setting can teach about the resilience of nature. Here you can see both exhibits and actual evidence of nature at work.

Dotting the Ohio & Erie Canal Reservation are patches of land that have bounced back from the clear-cutting of the area by the early settlers of the Western Reserve. Former farmlands have reverted to brush, meadow, and forest. The park also contains ponds, wetlands and stands of older-growth oaks, elms, cottonwoods, and maples. Although small and fragmented, these diverse habitats, in combination with the river and the watered canal, are an oasis for resident and migrating wildlife.

Good neighbors. Five nearby corporations and industries donated land to enable creation of the reservation. The East 49th Street plant of benefactor Birmingham Steel Company is pictured here.

Beaver, muskrat, deer, red fox, and coyote have been spotted here. Pushed out of their accustomed habitats by the onrush of development, they are drawn to "these little pockets of wild space like magnets," park naturalist Jenny McClain has observed. That's a bit of an understatement. With the help of amateur bird watchers, Cleveland Metroparks staff have counted no fewer than 350 varieties of birds that live or nest in the new reservation, or that rest there temporarily during spring and fall migrations. This impressively long list encompasses wading birds such as the great blue heron and the less well-known green heron, predators such as red-tailed and broad-winged hawks, and songbirds such as mockingbirds, a Southern species, and great crested flycatchers, a tropical migrant.

One of the songbirds, the yellow warbler, has been adopted as the park's unofficial mascot and goodwill ambassador. The choice was motivated in part because the yellow warbler's rapid, cheerful call—*sweet sweet oh so sweet*—and intense color make it appealing and easy to recognize. The yellow warbler also has an important story to tell: a story of survival against increasing odds. As more and more North American woodland gives way to subdivisions and shopping malls, this five-inch-long bird has been able—so far—to adapt to this loss of habitat and to continue to breed on the edges of increasingly fragmented forests.

Yellow warblers appear in the Ohio & Erie Canal Reservation as early as the third week in April, having migrated from their winter homes in the rain forests of Central and South America, a habitat that is also imperiled. (To counter this trend, Cleveland Metroparks has entered into a formal partnership with the Parque Natural Metropolitano in Panama City,

Fascinating rhythms. The reservation's educational programs illuminate the broad sweep of the Cuyahoga River Valley's economic history.

and has sent its professional staff down to the other end of the yellow warbler's migratory route to train, counsel, and learn from their Panamanian counterparts.)

On reaching the reservation, the first order of business for a male warbler—identifiable by the red streaks on his breast—is to establish his territory by outsinging larger birds. He then collaborates with his mate to build a nest in the forest understory. The female typically lays four to five eggs, which hatch in eleven days. Being insect eaters, the yellow warblers and their young have left the park and migrated south by the time of the first frost. The navigational guides they use on their 4,500-mile journey over land remain a mystery.

Appreciating how far the yellow warbler has flown to mate in his natal territory adds to the thrill of spotting a yellow glint in the bare branches during a spring bird walk in the park. For the lucky wildlife observer, spring also brings the chance to view an animal on the state of Ohio's "special-interest" list of potentially endangered species. Springtime visitors who walk along the Towpath Trail beside the murky waters of the canal should be on the watch for . . . turtles!?

Several species of these amphibious reptiles live in the environs of the canal, which has water cleaner than that of the river. The common varieties of turtle include painted, snapping, musk, and Eastern spiny, as well as red-eared sliders, the kind sold in pet stores, that have been abandoned by their owners. That land reclaimed from industry seems to support

Nature at work. Patches of meadows and woods scattered throughout this gritty industrial setting, as well as the watered section of the canal, harbor an astonishing abundance of wildlife.

a greater diversity of turtles than any other "Emerald Necklace" reservation came as a pleasant surprise to the Cleveland Metroparks natural resources staff engaged in a long-term research survey of frog, toad, salamander, and turtle populations in the park district. Imagine the researchers' delight when they discovered a rare species of turtle basking near the canal in the spring of 1999.

It was the bright yellow neck and smooth, dome-shaped shell that told park district research assistant Mark Skowronski that he was looking at a Blanding's turtle. "Your heart starts pounding when you see something this rare," remembers Skowronski, who had recently earned a degree in environmental science from Dennison University. He ran a half mile to his car to retrieve his camera. Without documentation no one would believe his sighting. Common wisdom held that this once prevalent species had been largely extirpated from this portion of the state.

Since cold-blooded turtles need to warm themselves after a winter's hibernation in the muddy bottom of ponds, the arrival of sunny days had lured the Blanding's turtle into the open. In another few weeks, when his body temperature had risen high enough to enable digestion, he would enter the canal to hunt for crayfish and would be more difficult to spot. During this small window of opportunity, Cleveland Metroparks researchers kept vigilant watch and spotted two, three, and then four Blanding's turtles simultaneously.

Eureka! Metroparks personnel were pleasantly surprised to discover that the reservation's wetlands are inhabited by a breeding population of rare Blanding's turtles.

Previous to the Canal Reservation sightings, the western Lake Erie marshes were the only locale in Ohio known to support a sizeable population of this rare species. When Skowronski succeeded in capturing a female and then a male Blanding's turtle that had overwintered in the park, he recorded their measurements and glued transmitters to their backs so that their movements could be tracked via radio telemetry. Now Cleveland Metroparks may be able to tell us more about the habits and life cycle of these uncommon animals. How far do the adults venture from their overwintering pond in their search for marshy summer shelter? Do they travel over land or make use of the canal? Is this a breeding population? (Blanding's turtles mate at the relatively advanced age of fifteen, which helps to explain why they could be in peril of becoming extinct. Wetlands destruction may be another reason.)

In June 2000, when the female laid twelve eggs, the park district gained the opportunity to conduct even more exacting research. Staffers shielded the nest from predatory raccoons and skunks and received permission from the state to raise six of the hatchlings for two years before releasing them back into the park. The other four hatchlings (two eggs did not hatch) were immediately released, so that their struggle for survival could be monitored and better understood.

Although people do not immediately think of parks as scientific laboratories, research is an important part of the educational mission of most large park systems. Cleveland Metroparks is no exception. Park visitors are beneficiaries of the park district's multifaceted research agenda. Reports from the field are shared with staff naturalists, who glean insights and colorful stories that can be incorporated into their talks and programs. Every species of flora and fauna within the system's boundaries will benefit from the frog and turtle survey being conducted in cooperation with Hugh Quinn, Cleveland Metroparks Zoo curator of zoological programs. Because the number and health of amphibians in a particular area are leading indicators of environmental quality (in that frogs and turtles inhabit both water and land), the knowledge gained from Dr. Quinn's survey will inform the park district's ongoing efforts to conserve the precious habitats in, and sometimes adjacent to, its reservations.

Indeed, conservation of the wild and scenic valleys of the rivers that drain into Lake Erie on either side of Cleveland was the objective behind the creation of the park district in 1917.

The idea is said to have been suggested first by Union general William Tecumseh Sherman on a post–Civil War visit to Cleveland. Taken out to admire the views in the Rocky River Valley, Sherman expressed his hope that the picturesque landscape would be set aside as a park so that its beauty might be preserved for generations to come. In 1905 William A. Stinchcomb, the city's chief engineer of parks, raised the issue again, to greater effect. In his annual report for that year Stinchcomb presciently observed:

> Through the valleys of Rocky River on the west, and Chagrin River on the east, lie some of the finest stretches of natural park lands to be found in the northern part of Ohio. While all this is now entirely outside of the city, it will be but a short time before they will be inside or very near the limits of a "Greater Cleveland" and it seems to me that such fine stretches of natural parkway should be secured for the benefit of the entire public before private enterprise or commercial industry places them beyond reach.

Stinchcomb's vision moved one step closer to reality in 1911, when state legislators approved a bill authorizing the creation of county park boards that could accept gifts of property.

Subsequently asked by the Cuyahoga County park board to design an outlying parks system, Stinchcomb drew inspiration from the work of America's greatest landscape architect, Frederick Law Olmsted, who in the late 1860s had first conceived the "emerald necklace" system of spacious parks connected by broad boulevards in responding to the developmental needs of the city of Buffalo. Stinchcomb brought Olmsted's son, who was carrying on his father's landscape architecture business, to Cleveland for a three-day tour of Cuyahoga County in 1915. Olmsted Jr.'s observations heavily influenced the master plan, *Cuyahoga County Park and Boulevard System,* that Stinchcomb presented the following year. It envisioned a continuous parkway, studded with "wild, wooded and isolated reservations," that would encircle Cuyahoga County as it snaked its way through the Rocky River, Big Creek, Chippewa Creek, Tinker's Creek, Chagrin River, and Euclid Creek valleys. In another progressive touch, the plan contemplated linkages with two Cleveland municipal parks: Edgewater and Brooklyn (now Brookside). But, visionary though they were in tracing the broad outlines of one of America's first *metropolitan* park systems, Olmsted Jr. and Stinchcomb apparently concurred that the county's premier river valley, the Cuyahoga, was too industrialized to save.

Stinchcomb served as the first director of Cleveland Metroparks, from 1921 to 1957, and during the Depression he attempted to rectify this oversight by proposing to the federal Works Progress Administration (WPA) that it undertake the construction of a parkway leading from Public Square through the Cuyahoga River Valley all the way to downtown Akron. Although WPA funding and Civilian Conservation Corps labor built many of the early roads, trails, and comfort and recreational facilities in the park district, this particular asset was to remain only a beautiful dream.

It would fall to the present-day administration of Cleveland Metroparks executive director-secretary Vern J. Hartenburg to secure a northern section of the Cuyahoga River Valley in the mid-1990s for the permanent enjoyment of the public. Keenly aware that citizens living in the center of the county were forced to drive some distance to reach an outlying Cleveland Metroparks reservation, the Hartenburg administration recognized that several conditions favored bold action to fill this gap in service. First, there was the popularity of Garfield Park Reservation. Under the terms of a long-term lease, Cleveland Metroparks had taken over management of this declining urban park from the city of Cleveland in 1986 and restored it over the course of several years. The experience "taught us that a park didn't have to be rough-hewn and rural to be a success," says Steve Coles, Cleveland Metroparks chief of park planning.

Second, interest in the Cuyahoga River Valley had heightened as a result of the regional effort to establish the Cleveland-to-Zoar portion of the Ohio & Erie Canal as a National Heritage Corridor. As part of the preparation of a new master plan, the park district began its own exploration of whether industry and recreation could coexist in the valley. When Tom Tyrrell, then new as president of American Steel & Wire, and an avid runner who had enjoyed living near a Heritage Corridor in Illinois, approached Cleveland Metroparks to lobby for the Ohio Corridor undertaking, he found a receptive audience. The park district's administration accepted Tyrrell's offer to convene a meeting between Cleveland Metroparks and the leaders of the Aluminum Company of America (ALCOA), BP America, Cleveland Electric Illuminating Company, and the regional sewer district, all of which had operations in the valley near American Steel & Wire (now Birmingham Steel).

These discussions ultimately blossomed into a precedent-setting partnership. The land needed for creation of the Ohio & Erie Canal Reservation was pieced together primarily through easements and lease agreements with the help of the five companies at the table and the Ohio Department of Natural Resources, which provided the canal's sixty-six-acre right-of-way. State and federal officials contributed financial resources to the $10 million project. For example, the U.S. Department of Transportation awarded Cleveland Metroparks nearly $2 million to build the park's 4.3-mile stretch of the Towpath Trail, an extension of

On the Towpath Trail. Canal Reservation boasts a 4.3-mile extension of the Cuyahoga River Valley's popular new transportation artery.

Observing Nature at Work

Pent-up demand. South Side Clevelanders appreciate having a conveniently located Cleveland Metroparks reservation.

the 20-mile hiking and biking path that runs alongside the canal in the Cuyahoga Valley National Park.

More than 25,000 people participated in the opening-weekend festivities at the Ohio & Erie Canal Reservation in 1999—proof that Cleveland Metroparks planners had been right about pent-up demand for a centrally located reservation. Almost as soon as the new asphalt cooled on the extension of the valley's newest transportation artery, joggers and bikers discovered it, and the Towpath Trail in the reservation has been busy ever since. Today, in good and bad weather, the trail attracts a stream of cyclists, runners, in-line skaters, and walkers. Who knows? Research may one day reveal that the hiking and biking path is popular even with Blanding's turtles.

MILL CREEK FALLS
PARK & TRAIL

Pathway to Revitalization

CLEVELAND'S BROADWAY NEIGHBORHOOD

Imagine stepping outside your home and finding yourself, after less than a five-minute walk, on a hiking and biking trail that connects you to a world of natural and cultural attractions. Walk in one direction down the trail and you soon come to a Cleveland Metroparks reservation, where you can picnic or play baseball or continue your stroll.

Walk in the other direction and you arrive at a rustic pavilion overlooking a stream that runs through your neighborhood, where you can relax and take in the beauty of an unexpected waterfall. If you are interested in local history, a small museum operated by your neighborhood historical society is open for exploration in a nearby century home. Or, if you have brought your bike, you can easily pedal over to the Towpath Trail on a connecting path leading from the waterfall's scenic overlook. And, once you are on the Towpath Trail (which will one day follow the course of the old Ohio & Erie Canal for one hundred miles from New Philadelphia, Ohio, to downtown Cleveland), you will be able to get to almost any park, preserve, or point of interest in northeast Ohio's expanding emerald network without having to hop into your car.

Sound too good to be true?

Not to the residents of the Broadway neighborhood on Cleveland's South Side. Such

Not your typical subdivision. Residents of Mill Creek Homes, the largest single-family residential development built in the city of Cleveland since World War II, gather for a memorial tree-planting ceremony at their handsome community center.

an attractive, "smart-growth" scenario is close to becoming a reality for the thirty thousand people who live in this inner-city neighborhood. A once-thriving enclave of Irish, Polish, and Czech immigrants drawn by jobs in a steel mill located in the neighborhood, Broadway is fighting its way back from a decline precipitated by the city's loss of manufacturing strength in the last quarter of the twentieth century. Tangible evidence of the community's turnaround can be seen in the first mile and a half of a new hiking and biking trail that opened for public use in 1999 along the banks of Mill Creek in the southeastern corner of Broadway. Tree-shaded and inviting, this section of the creek had formerly been off limits because it ran through the grounds of a state hospital for mentally and developmentally disabled persons. Kids who ventured onto the property to go exploring after the hospital closed in the late 1980s risked being chased away by security guards.

Today Mill Creek Trail rewards those who follow it with an unimpeded view of the creek, an important tributary of the Cuyahoga River. And, at trail's end, they gain convenient entrée to the upper level of Garfield Reservation (formerly Garfield Park, now a unit of Cleveland Metroparks) in neighboring Garfield Heights. This is no small reward.

One of the parks created in celebration of Cleveland's centennial, the 177-acre Garfield Reservation merits increased attention, as it is notable for its historic origins, its dramatic topography, and its meticulous upkeep. The park was established on the outskirts of Cleve-

Rooms with a view. Homes in Broadway's new market-rate subdivision overlook historic Mill Creek and a new hike and bike path that opened along a 1.5-mile stretch of its banks in 1999. Home buyers have beautified the trail by planting trees.

land in 1896, on farmland chosen because it harbored high wooded promontories and Mill and Wolf Creeks. At its peak in the years following the Depression, when it had been the beneficiary of the ministrations of the Work Projects Administration, Garfield Park contained eight baseball diamonds, seven tennis courts, a football field, and an outdoor swimming pool and bathhouse. The upper of its two artificial lakes, created by the damming of Wolf Creek, was stocked with fish and outfitted with a fly-casting peninsula. The lower lake, used for boating since the turn of the twentieth century (when you could rent a canoe and a paddle for ten cents; if you wanted two paddles, it would cost you a dime more), had recently been enhanced by the addition of a colonnaded stone boathouse approached by an arched stone footbridge. It could now lay claim to being the most picturesque boating lagoon around.

Garfield Park's luster began to diminish in the 1970s. The fact that the park was owned by the city of Cleveland but located in Garfield Heights gave rise to jurisdictional disputes and budget reductions that adversely affected the property's maintenance. Over time, vandals reduced the boathouse to a swastika-scarred ruin, and the lakes became unsightly dumping grounds. At one point the pockmarked condition of the park roads necessitated the posting of a sign advising visitors "Travel at Your Own Risk."

Making an investment. Mill Creek Homes took off in a neighborhood that has seen better days because it offered something nearly eight out of ten prospective home buyers consider important: easy access to parks and natural open spaces. Annual trash roundups are a tangible demonstration of the neighborhood's green priorities.

This period of neglect ended in 1986, when the park was leased by Cleveland Metroparks, a move that quashed suggestions that the property should be sold to the highest bidder. Although Cleveland Metroparks had not previously managed an urban park like Garfield (which differed from a typically rustic reservation in boasting such old-fashioned detailing as flagstone walkways and such modern touches as roadside curbing), the park district's rehabilitation of Garfield Reservation has been both sensitive and sensible. Since only extensive dredging and future improvements in water quality can make the lower lake once again suitable for boating, it has been managed in the interim as a wetland wildlife sanctuary. Although the signature boathouse was deemed to be beyond repair, a new nature center is a more than adequate replacement, offering educational programming as well as activities and entertainment. Hand-cut stone stairs built to last by the Civilian Conservation Corps lead up the promontories to well-graveled paths winding through magnificent stands of century-old trees and past a playing field that has been allowed to revert to a wildflower meadow.

Cleveland Metroparks also built and maintains Mill Creek Trail, the first phase of a thirty-five-acre parklands development which is restoring a corridor of green along the creek after it exits Garfield Reservation on its eleven-mile journey to the Cuyahoga River. A master plan prepared at the request of the Broadway Area Housing Coalition by Schmidt Copeland Parker Stevens, a Cleveland architecture and landscape architecture firm, also

Trail's end. Mill Creek Homes is connected, via the new bike path, to Garfield Reservation. One of the large municipal parks created to celebrate Cleveland's centennial, the reservation is notable for its dramatic topography and handsome stonework.

called for the creation of a small nature preserve near Garfield Reservation through which a loop of the new trail runs. Now completed, Phase I of the plan cost approximately $300,000.

Phase II, completed at a cost of $1.4 million, extended the trail to the point at which the creek abruptly drops forty-five feet. Here a scenic overlook and visitors center allow full enjoyment of the tallest waterfall in Cuyahoga County. The Northeast Ohio Regional Sewer District has agreed to reroute and seal a combined sewer overflow valve atop the falls as part of a $126 million modernization and flood control program for Cuyahoga County.

Until its rediscovery and proposed reclamation by the Broadway Area Housing Coalition (BAHC, which has since merged with a community development corporation to become Slavic Village Development) and the public-private partnership BAHC forged to carry out the redevelopment project, the waterfall had been hidden from view by a century's accumulation of buildings, roadways, railroad tracks, and bridges. As a consequence, few northern Ohioans know about this impressive natural attraction. And, even among present-day Broadway residents, there is only dim awareness of the past economic significance of the pioneer settlement of Newburgh that sprang up around the falls.

Exercising care. The rehabilitation of once-neglected Garfield Reservation has been both sensitive and sensible. In the upper level of the reservation, a playing field has been allowed to revert to a wildflower meadow.

The Mill Creek redevelopment project may provide the impetus to recapture this underappreciated chapter in the history of the Western Reserve. Slavic Village Development and the Slavic Village Historical Society hope to open an interpretive center in the former Brilla House, built in 1888 and located near the site of the Mill Creek Falls Park scenic overlook. Exhibits will trace the waterfall's role in Newburgh's development, a story that begins in 1799.

That year, the Connecticut Land Company paid William N. Williams and Major Ezra Wyatt $150 to start a gristmill powered by Mill Creek falls in the hopes that the availability of such a service would speed sales of Western Reserve land to farmers. Unfortunately, the entrepreneurs' decision to locate the mill at the base of the falls generated more complaints than profits from customers whose flour and meal returned to them slightly damp. The operation was soon relocated above the falls, where it was subsequently joined by a sawmill and a carding mill.

So equipped, Newburgh grew faster than its neighbor, Cleveland, six miles away. The sawmill produced the lumber used to build the first frame home in the county, while the gristmill made possible the establishment of a distillery. The manufacture of mill-ground corn whiskey in Newburgh is said to have been Cuyahoga County's first industry. These enterprises, in turn, sparked the construction of a coach road along an old Indian trail that was later named Broadway Avenue.

The transformation of a brownfield. To facilitate the development of Mill Creek Falls Park & Trail, Slavic Village Development Corporation (SVDC) assumed responsibility for effecting the environmental remediation of the thirty-five-acre site. SVDC's Bobbi Reichtell, far right, offers instruction and encouragement to volunteers who help to keep the new parklands clean.

By 1809 Newburgh felt sufficiently prosperous to challenge its neighbor to the north in an election to become county seat. Although it lost this honor, Newburgh continued to thrive. In 1855 Thomas Garfield, uncle of President James A. Garfield, donated fifty acres of land to the state of Ohio to establish a "lunatic asylum" within Newburgh's confines. For more than 130 years the state operated a mental health facility on the site, which eventually doubled in size.

Newburgh's selection as the location for an iron mill was to prove a greater boon. The Cleveland Rolling Mill Company, which specialized in railroad iron, went on to become an early manufacturer of steel "bricks." Later the company diversified into wire, screws, and nuts and ultimately became part of U.S. Steel. When Newburgh was annexed by Cleveland in 1875, people naturally began to refer to it as the city's "iron ward." The name also seems

Gateway to the regional parks network. Mill Creek Trail eventually will be extended south to hook up via a connector in Bacci Park to the Towpath Trail. This development will bring Broadway into the orbit of the Ohio & Erie Canal National Heritage Corridor, another potentially revitalizing influence.

to have been attached to Iron Spring, a popular mineral-water seep located in Garfield Park near the last stop of the Broadway Avenue trolley line. (It is said that Clevelanders once came from far and wide, containers in hand, to avail themselves of the spring waters. Iron Spring can still be seen, although it has been reduced to a rusty trickle.)

In the third phase of the new parklands project, Mill Creek Trail will be extended farther south to hook up with a new hiking and biking path built by Cuyahoga Heights in Bacci Park. The Bacci trail ties into the Towpath Trail in the Ohio & Erie Canal Reservation, the newest Cleveland Metroparks unit. Thus, the ailing Broadway neighborhood will soon be linked to the Ohio & Erie Canal National Heritage Corridor, another potentially revitalizing influence. The Cuyahoga County Planning Commission has estimated that, once it is made accessible, Mill Creek Falls Park & Trail could annually attract as many as fifty thousand visitors. The influx of sightseers is expected to prompt the creation of new businesses serving their needs and to swell the revenues of Broadway's existing retailers and restaurants.

History testifies to the popularity of the falls as a tourist draw. In pre–Civil War times young men and women flocked on weekends to the Eagle Hotel located nearby at Broadway and Miles to twirl around on a cushioned dance floor (it was built on springs) and sample the house speciality: nut cakes fried in bear grease. The Cataract (later Spencer) House, a hotel located directly above the falls, operated well into the twentieth century.

Hidden treasure. In Phase II of Slavic Village's redevelopment initiative Mill Creek Trail was extended to Mill Creek Falls Park, where a scenic overlook was built. Cuyahoga County's tallest waterfall has been obscured from public view by a century's accumulation of buildings, roadways, railroad tracks, and bridges.

Even in its earliest stages, Broadway's Mill Creek Falls Park & Trail has spurred new real estate and business development that would be the envy of any town. Like the history of Mill Creek falls, this impressive story of neighborhood renewal deserves to be better known throughout the region, as it may inspire other communities to conceive big plans for their open spaces and natural assets.

The story begins in the late 1980s, when Bobbi Reichtell, a community redevelopment activist, initiated a neighborhood discussion of the future of the abandoned state hospital site. Reichtell, a senior member of the staff of Broadway's housing development corporation, sought to prevent use of the land for a prison pre-release center or a juvenile-offender boot camp. Neither of these proposed options offered residents a reason to stay in the neighborhood, nor would they attract newcomers. Reichtell was tireless in presenting an alternative option—her vision of Mill Creek as a significant recreational resource that could be used to speed Broadway's economic redevelopment—to officials from the state of Ohio, the city of Cleveland, and other affected municipalities, Cleveland Metroparks representatives, philanthropic leaders, and Broadway residents. Partner by partner, she built a broad base of support for the parkway project.

After the state legislature passed enabling legislation turning over the hospital site to the housing development corporation in 1990, Reichtell issued a request for proposals from private developers interested in building market-rate homes on the property. In consultation with the above-named partners and a newly created citizen's advisory committee, Zaremba Cleveland Communities was chosen to build a new housing development on a fifty-eight-acre parcel of the hospital site that lay between Mill Creek and Turney Road, near the intersection of Broadway Avenue and Warner Road.

Mill Creek Homes was not to be a typical subdivision. Its name derived from a real and appealing feature of the landscape, not a flight of fancy. It was located, not on a bulldozed stretch of anonymous terrain, but in colorful "Old Newburgh," the second settlement in the Western Reserve. The construction of Mill Creek Homes would consume no woodlands or cornfields. Nor would its houses be strung out along a featureless cul-de-sac. Zaremba proposed to foster a small-town atmosphere by offering frame houses built on urban-size lots and individualized with architectural detailing from an earlier era, such as front porches and Victorian gingerbread. A grid of short streets would encourage strolling toward a common green topped by a contemporary-style gazebo, the perfect spot for a neighborly chat. (Proceeds from the sale of a seven-acre parcel of the former hospital site to a relocating business were used to underwrite the gazebo's construction costs.)

Yet none of these distinctions can fully explain Zaremba's astonishing success in attracting middle-class home buyers to a subdivision located in the central city. Within a year of the 1997 ground breaking for Mill Creek Homes, more than half of the lots in this planned community of 222 single-family houses had been sold. By the year 2000, 90 homes had been built, some with market values as high as $275,000. Almost overnight, Mill Creek Homes had become the largest single-family residential development built in the city of Cleveland since World War II.

In a section of Cleveland that had seen better days, the subdivision took off precisely because it offered something more than attractively designed housing at affordable prices, something that nearly eight out of ten prospective home buyers consider very important or even essential to their decision to live in a planned community. That special something was —just as Reichtell had envisioned—easy access to parks and natural open spaces.

The fact that Mill Creek Trail would link the subdivision to the Ohio & Erie Canal Reservation, a "gateway" to the growing regional parks network, constituted a powerful incentive to buy. "To succeed in the city, developers must strive to add to the fabric of the existing neighborhood," says Zaremba Cleveland Communities president Nate Zaremba. "Creating outdoor living rooms for everyone to enjoy is a really effective way of doing that."

Ironically, building Mill Creek Trail proved to be harder than selling it. The hospital site was essentially a brownfield, polluted by more than a mile of underground steam pipes wrapped in asbestos, three underground gasoline storage tanks, and an unauthorized 6.5-acre landfill containing construction and demolition debris studded with such institutional discards as old hospital beds, bathtubs, and wheelchairs. "I was near tears when I realized the magnitude of the problems," Reichtell remembers. It was especially upsetting to discover that the issue of environmental contamination posed an initial impediment to involvement by Cleveland Metroparks, a partnership that had first been urged by government officials in Garfield Heights impressed with the park district's stewardship of adjacent Garfield Reservation. To pave the way for Cleveland Metroparks to participate as manager of the desired trail and parklands, the development corporation assumed responsibility for remediation of the site.

The city of Cleveland supported that effort with a grant of $150,000, which paid for the surface cleanup of the landfill and its regrading and seeding. A contingent of two hundred volunteers from the neighborhood and the community at large planted one hundred mature trees. Recognizing that Cleveland Metroparks cannot use public monies to benefit a commercial enterprise directly, the George Gund Foundation, The Cleveland Foundation, and the Farnham Trust provided funds to construct the portion of Mill Creek Trail that runs behind the subdivision.

Experience has indeed proved that the value of adjoining properties skyrockets whenever and wherever green or open space is created. As far back as 1897, *Plain Dealer* publisher and Cleveland parks commission member Liberty F. Holden made that point to Cleveland City Council in arguing for public funding of parkways to connect the commission's holdings of large tracts on the outskirts on the city's East, West, and (with the recent purchase of property in Newburgh) South Sides. Having observed Central Park before and after its construction, Holden was able to report that:

> it was like a wilderness, a mass of rocks and ravines and springs, a dwelling place of squatters around whose cabins were clotheslines filled with red shirts, tattered linen, patched coats and trousers, and a thousand and one things from goats to donkey cars, wheelbarrows, picks, dilapidated wagons, as well as dilapidated men and women. Now it is a thing of beauty, it is a joy for all the people . . . [and] its influence on surrounding property has been the marvel of the age. . . . Already it is surrounded by the city, magnificent houses, towering apartment buildings, hotels that surpass any thing in all the world have been erected there until the property adjacent to Central Park and not very far distant therefrom has an assessable value greater than all New York had in 1850. . . . [C]onversion of lands to parks and boulevards has increased the value of surrounding property in all our cities where this has been carried out, from 300 to 500 percent. It will do the same for the City of Cleveland.

One hundred years later, Mill Creek Homes is another remarkable demonstration that parks are still working their magic as catalysts for neighborhood renewal and economic development.

HERSHEY CHILDREN'S GARDEN

Play That Educates

UNIVERSITY CIRCLE, CLEVELAND

"Every child should have mud pies, grasshoppers, waterbugs, tadpoles, frogs, mud turtles, elderberries, wild strawberries, acorns, chestnuts, trees to climb, brooks to wade, water lilies, woodchucks, bats, bees, butterflies, various animals to pet, hayfields, pine-cones, rocks to roll, sand, snakes, huckleberries and hornets," said the famed horticulturist and hybridizer Luther Burbank. Burbank died in the early years of the twentieth century, even as the great migration from farm to city was severing the intimate relationship that the majority of Americans enjoyed with the natural world.

Most adults and children today experience the great outdoors only on vacations or special-occasion outings. The isolation of urban kids from nature is practically total. Burbank believed that children who spend their growing-up years largely in manmade environments have missed out on "the best part of education," a philosophy with which the director of Cleveland Botanical Garden in University Circle wholeheartedly agreed.

Appointed in 1994, Brian E. Holley encouraged his staff and trustees to expand the institution's mission beyond service to garden enthusiasts. He pushed for the creation of educational programming aimed at providing urban dwellers with both the information and the inspiration needed to grow and harvest plants. Finding plans to create an on-site community

A new kind of green space. Ohio's first children's garden is at once a fantasy farm, interactive classroom, and ecological jungle gym.

garden already on the drawing board, Holley challenged his colleagues to push beyond the conventional.

Debra Hershey Guren, a new trustee of Cleveland Botanical Garden, strongly supported the idea of a children's garden. "For all sorts of reasons kids don't play outside as much today as they used to, and they're getting robbed of something important in their development," she believed. A children's garden where youngsters could get their hands dirty planting things and see the beautiful results would help combat this unfortunate trend. It would instill in them a love of gardening, just as the pansy bed that Guren's mother, Jo Hershey Seldon, had helped young Debra put in every spring had fostered a passion for plants in her daughter.

As there were few working models of Guren's concept, Cleveland Botanical Garden

It's a wonderful world. While its approach is playful, the garden has a serious objective. It seeks to foster in children an interest in plants, gardening, and the interconnectedness of nature.

staff and trustees recognized the need to locate an exceptional landscape architect. Herbert R. Schaal, a principal of EDAW, Inc., in Fort Collins, Colorado, was ultimately selected to lead a new design process. The creator of more than seventy-five public gardens and parks and winner of more than two dozen awards from the American Society of Landscape Architects, Schaal encouraged local students, teachers, artists, and specialists in child behavior to participate in his design workshops, as well as horticulturists, engineers, and Botanical Garden staff, trustees, and volunteers.

Untraditional though it may have been, this collaboration produced the first children's garden in Ohio. It also produced a comprehensive model for a new kind of green space—the play area that seeks to educate—that will surely influence the parks and recreation movement of the twenty-first century as it becomes better known.

Hershey Children's Garden was dedicated on June 25, 1999. The name honors the memory of Jo Hershey Selden and her husband, Alvin A. Hershey, whose children and family foundation were the major benefactors of the project. At once a fantasy farm, interactive classroom, and ecological jungle gym, Hershey Children's Garden is more fun than a bin full of earthworms. (Said bin, filled with soil in which the worms are busy bulldozing paths, is one of the garden's many unconventional displays.) Although an obvious objective of

"Wow." One section of the garden represents a regional Ohio landscape, complete with a pond, meadow, forest, and cave.

Hershey Children's Garden is to promote play, its underlying purpose is serious: to foster in children an interest in and appreciation for the world of plants, the value of gardening, and the interconnectedness of nature. The earthworms, for example, are a wonderfully icky way to illustrate the importance of nourishing and working the soil.

Much to everyone's relief, the garden was an immediate hit with its target audience—children aged six to eleven—as well as younger children and their families. On opening day tension was high as the garden's fanciful wrought-iron gates (created by Kent, Ohio, artist Brinsley Tyrell) were thrown open. Would all the carefully planned features work as intended? Two little girls in dresses came through the entry gates, which depict an enchanted landscape in which a mammoth butterfly and a variety of garden insects live, and ran right over to Picnic Hill, a turf-covered knoll meant to encourage toddlers to test out their motor

Pint-sized challenges. The topographic features in the garden encourage independent exploration and self-discovery.

skills. Climbing to the top of Picnic Hill, the girls hesitated only a moment before they began rolling down the modest slope, skirts flying.

"Wow," garden benefactor Debra Hershey Guren exulted, "it works!" A Montessori advocate with a master's degree in education, Guren is extremely sensitive to children's frustration with the oversize scale of the adult world and was vigilant about the issue as it played out day by day in the construction of the garden. Concerned with the user-friendliness of every make-believe prop from the bird blind to the tool shed, she immediately recognized that a prefab cottage ordered for the garden was too big. Her suggestion: Cut eighteen inches from the bottom to make it a less-intimidating height.

Grownup visitors to the garden were also instantly smitten by its pint-sized scale. Some bemoaned their inability to use the kids' entrances: two cunning, vine-covered tunnels flanking the main gate that are four feet tall at most. Others oohed and aahed over all the whimsical touches: the flowers growing on the roof of the cottage, the birdhouses with tin roofs made from old license plates, the little benches and tables fashioned from tree stumps, the petunias sprouting in discarded high-heeled shoes in the Scrounger's Garden (a feature meant to demonstrate that plants can be grown successfully in almost any container). Buoyed by favorable word of mouth about the unpredictable attractions waiting to be discovered

Water as kid magnet. Few visitors can resist the invitation to fill a watering can at one of the garden's old-fashioned hand pumps and tend to the dazzling array of flowers.

beyond each turn of the path in the half-acre garden, attendance swelled to more than a hundred thousand during the first two years of operation.

Although Hershey Children's Garden feels as spontaneous as laughter, it is organized into three formal sections. Each aims to stimulate all of a child's senses as the best means of promoting learning. Docents and groundskeepers (the latter dressed like farmers in bib overalls and straw hats) are on hand to answer questions, and there are formal educational programs for school classes and regular public events such as cider pressings. But, most importantly, Hershey Children's Garden rewards independent exploration and self-discovery.

Beyond the entrance (where the Luther Burbank quote that opens this chapter has been carved into the pavement in a child's handwriting) lies the Four Seasons Court, a section that promotes awareness of the earth's natural cycles and changing seasons. The design of Herb Schaal as interpreted by Cleveland sculptor Mary Wayrytko, the circular plaza is embedded with an array of images with a graphic appeal that belies their educational mission: compass points; the phases of the moon; the days, months, and seasons of the year. At the center of the plaza is a sundial with bronze sun face and red stone rays. The sun's mouth spouts a jet of water at erratic intervals, compelling nearly every child who enters the garden to draw near and await his chance to touch the spray or run through it.

Hershey Children's Garden

Sun worship. Activities and imagery in the Four Seasons Court at the garden's entrance are aimed at promoting awareness of the earth's natural cycles and changing seasons.

The Four Seasons Court offers a picture-perfect view of the one feature desired by every child who participated in Schaal's design workshops: a gigantic wooden treehouse, which has been built around two mature tulip poplar trees at the northernmost end of the garden. A curved path leading to the treehouse is imprinted with the "footprints" of woodland animals: a rabbit here, a blue heron there. Is that a fox track up ahead? The path leads along a newly created stream and mill run that are part of the ecological section of the garden. Here visitors find a representation of a regional Ohio landscape—complete with a pond, wetland, bog, meadow, forest, cliffs, and cave, and the plant communities appropriate to these native habitats.

Interestingly, kids climb the curved wooden staircase to the treehouse deck seven feet above the ground, survey the premises, and immediately return to earth. Maybe it's too

Tea for two. The garden's design team has been sensitive to children's frustration with the oversize scale of the adult world.

quiet up there. They prefer to clamber up the cliff face behind the treehouse or jump from steppingstone to steppingstone across the pond at its foot. In addition to a beaver lodge and a floating raft (loosely tethered to prevent wild rocking), the four-foot-deep pond now sports a "No Swimming" sign. On opening day, kids jumped right into the millstream.

Water is a kid magnet, that's for sure. The most popular features of the horticultural section (in the southeastern part of Hershey Children's Garden) are three old-fashioned hand pumps, painted bright red. Even toddlers like to carry plastic watering cans over to a pump to be filled. If they sprinkle the ground instead of the flower boxes on the windows of the cottage, they aren't scolded. After all, the purpose of the horticultural section is to encourage hands-on learning. Among the many subgardens located here are a five-row corn-field, an orchard (apple trees having been high on the wish list of the young design consult-

Her very own secret garden. As the famed horticulturist and hybridizer Luther Burbank once observed, an intimate relationship with living things is "the best part of education."

ants), a vegetable patch, and an herb garden. Children are invited to tend and harvest the bounty of each.

"Let's go into the vegetable garden," a Cleveland Botanical Garden education department member suggested to a kindergarten class from Shaker Heights, Ohio, that was visiting one late fall afternoon. "We don't have enough produce for everyone to pick, but I'm going to let you take home something that will make your food taste and smell good."

The staffer led the kindergartners over to a clump of basil. "Here, smell this," she said, breaking off a few basil leaves and passing them around. "You can put it in spaghetti sauce."

"We have it in pesto," a five-year-old sophisticate piped.

The afternoon's session concluded in the activity garden, where the kindergartners were given black plastic seedling pots and three wax bean seeds. After ladling soil into the pots, the kids were instructed to poke three holes in the loam with the tip of an index finger and drop in the seeds, which were big enough to have germinated Jack's beanstalk. They covered and watered the seeds and then stuck wooden markers, on which they had laboriously printed their names, into the pots so that they could be accurately redistributed upon the class's return to school.

No doubt this was a positive first experience with horticulture for many of these youngsters. With an expanded array of community and school gardening projects, Cleveland Botanical Garden is helping to turn a general unfamiliarity with plants into knowledgeability, a lack of interest into delight. And now, thanks to the collective vision of the organization's board, staff, and professional design team, it has given those area children who live apart from nature their very own secret garden. One can only hope that the seeds planted there may someday produce more than yellow beans. Perhaps some of the children who visit Hershey Children's Garden will take away a lesson or two—about the joy and beauty of living things and the rewards that come with nurturing and patience—that will blossom into an enduring concern for the greening of their corner of Greater Cleveland.

FOREST HILLS PARK

Programmed to Succeed

CLEVELAND'S GLENVILLE NEIGHBORHOOD

At Forest Hills Park in Glenville, the picnic pavilion sits next to the basketball and tennis courts. On a Saturday evening in early spring, the basketball courts are packed. Five years ago young men playing hoops would have been the only people using the park, a long, winding green space that follows the culverted watercourse of Dugway Creek as it passes through Glenville on its way to Lake Erie. For many years the other residents of this East Side Cleveland neighborhood reluctantly shunned their nearly century-old community park. Because of the tough language and demeanor of the guys who hung out at the basketball courts, and the run-down condition of Forest Hills Park itself, parents forbade their children to play there and avoided it themselves.

Given the effort that originally went into creating the park, which is located roughly between Eddy Road on the east, Lakeview Road on the west, the East Cleveland city line on the south, and the Memorial Shoreway on the north, this was an especially unfortunate turn of events. Forest Hills Park was established as the final act of the administration of Cleveland mayor Tom L. Johnson. Interestingly, the land was not purchased by the city parks commission, nor was it given to the public by a single wealthy individual (as was the case with Forest Hill Park, John D. Rockefeller's gift to the citizens of East Cleveland and Cleveland

Climbing back from neglect. Once unkempt and unsafe, Forest Hills Park has been revitalized by a ParkWorks initiative that involved Glenville residents in determining capital and programmatic improvements.

Heights). It was donated by a number of average Cleveland citizens, who were inspired to turn over a portion of their backyards—the steep hillsides running down to Dugway Creek—for the common use of the neighborhood. It took the city more than twenty years to turn the narrow parkway into viable recreational space, as polluted Dugway Creek first had to be culverted and then filled in. After living with the stench from the open creek for the twelve years that elapsed before Dugway was culverted, Glenville residents then endured infestations of rats drawn by five more years of rubbish- and dirt-dumping, a necessary tactic for creating level land on which to build a swimming pool, baseball diamonds, playgrounds, and picnic areas.

Although immediately popular, these facilities were allowed to decline during the last years of the century as the municipal park budget was slashed and slashed again in response to the slow erosion of Cleveland's tax base. City finances eventually rebounded, but the deterioration of Forest Hills Park seemed unstoppable. By the mid-1990s, the park lacked even such basics as well-marked entrances and places to sit or gather, to say nothing of such niceties as family-oriented programming. Outsiders understandably might have mistaken some sections of the ill-tended parkway for vacant land. Worshipers attending Sunday services at several adjacent churches felt free to park their cars on its grounds every week, a

Signs of caring. A community vigil that kicked off a safe summer in the park offered neighborhood kids a chance to have their faces painted.

telling sign that residents lacked pride in Forest Hills Park—or perhaps even that they were unaware of its existence.

But that was five years ago. On the evening of Saturday, May 6, 2000, Forest Hills Park looks well-tended. Many of its recreational amenities have been restored. The picnic pavilion is even busier than the recently resurfaced basketball courts. Gathered inside are dozens of children, including a few babies in arms, and their parents, a contingent of older women from the neighborhood, and a smattering of young adults. They have all come out to "kick off a safe summer in Forest Hills Park," by participating in a "community vigil," as the event has been billed by its sponsor, the "Parks for People" initiative. Supported by a four-year grant of $423,700 from the Lila Wallace–Reader's Digest Fund of New York, the initiative sought to encourage stewardship of Forest Hills Park and other neglected, under-utilized neighborhood parks in Cleveland by involving their constituents in decision making about parks programming and redevelopment. It has been the catalytic force behind the rebirth of Forest Hills Park.

The community vigil marked the start of the fourth summer in which Parks for People organized a variety of park programs, such as a kite-making workshop, an arts festival, and a regular story-time hour, to meet the express wishes of residents. Throughout the vigil the picnic pavilion reverberates with the beat of world drums played by three musicians dressed

Programmed to Succeed

Unexpected outcome. With crime down in Forest Hills Park, Cleveland police have more time for building relation- ships with its patrons.

in colorful kente cloth. The children are invited to pick up a bell, a rattle, or a tambourine and join in. Others have their faces painted or learn how to make sweet-smelling sachets to give to their moms on Mother's Day. Some kids play on a brand-new jungle gym, while others crowd around two mounted police, patting their horses. Two community policemen, clad in shorts, are there on bikes. The presence of the four officers is yet more evidence that some- body *truly cares* about the eighty-eight-acre park.

While the kids line up for treats, the adults are content to sit and socialize. Vera Porter, an avid home redecorator who lives near East 95th Street and St. Clair Avenue, is there to offer craft lessons because she worries that "kids are losing their ability to work with their hands." Another woman has come all the way from a public housing project across town to show ten youngsters—her grandchildren and their friends—a good time. Evelyn Jones, a senior citizen, presides over a display promoting this year's Health Walk, a Parks for People program that challenges neighborhood residents to walk fifteen miles in fifteen days through Forest Hills Park. Jones and another older woman are wearing "Fun & Fitness" T-shirts they earned by completing Health Walks the previous summer. Both women are active mem- bers of the Friends of Forest Hills Park and Parkway.

"I've lived in Glenville all my life," Jones's friend observes. "For a while there, people ignored or ran away from problems in the park."

Forest Hills Park

Beautification project. A new entrance to the park was constructed and landscaped in a single weekend by two hundred volunteers from the immediate neighborhood and the larger Cleveland community.

"Yeah, remember when it was just a field of dirt?" Jones asks.

"Then we decided to meet the problem head on," the other woman continues. "Now a lot of people are doing things, even little things, to make it theirs.

"I'm a product of this city," she adds, explaining her commitment to the park. "Why should I leave it?"

The Parks for People Initiative sprang from a Community Design Day organized in 1995 by the Cleveland office of the Trust for Public Land and Clean-Land, Ohio, a not-for-profit agency with more than two decades of experience in urban beautification, environmental education, and reforestation. In order to act on the ideas, and keep alive the hopes, for Forest Hills's renewal generated at the brainstorming session, Clean-Land (renamed ParkWorks when its mission expanded to include strengthening urban parks and recreation) had set about building long-term collaborative relationships with neighborhood activists and institutions found in and around the park. The staff of ParkWorks began attending Ward 9 club meetings of Cleveland city councilman Craig Willis. They also sat in on the Saturday morning get-togethers of the Friends of Forest Hills Park and Parkway, an ad hoc support group formed at the behest of Willis. Months of discussion produced an ambitious rescue plan.

To start with, the new Parks for People partnership decided to create simple gardens at park entrances, particularly those spots with illegal dumping problems or where the dead ends of streets opened onto the grounds. A tree lawn garden soon bloomed at the southern terminus of East 117 Street. The neighbors who had participated in this beautification project subsequently organized a garden club that met biweekly.

More elaborate, terraced entry gardens were also planned, both to boost the park's appearance and to provide casual seating. In the spring of 1998 a landscaped terrace was built in one weekend at the park's Whitmore Avenue entrance with $35,000 in donated materials and the labor of two hundred volunteers from the immediate neighborhood and the larger Cleveland community. ParkWorks' Young Leadership Council had coordinated the undertaking. The next fall many of the volunteers, including a large number of neighborhood residents and children, returned to the Whitmore garden to weed, prune, and plant flower bulbs.

Northeastern Neighborhood Development Corporation, a not-for-profit organization working to encourage reinvestment in Cleveland's Glenville, Forest Hills, and Collinwood communities, organized block clubs on streets with homes that backed up to Forest Hills Park rather than facing it. In addition to preventing illegal dumping that took place in the park when "no one was watching," block club members participated in park cleanups that also attracted volunteers from Cleveland's Americorp bank and Case Western Reserve University. The Glenville Recreation Center and the Glenville YM-YWCA collaborated with ParkWorks on launching, respectively, an annual Make-a-Kite Clinic and the Health Walk Challenge, while the Greater Friendship Baptist Church volunteered to host the first two Worship in the Park services. Each service began with a procession of rousing gospel singers, who led parishioners to the park, where a large tent had been erected, and concluded with an old-fashioned ice cream social. The two events attracted one thousand participants and made a sufficiently emphatic statement about the value of the park to put an end to the illegal car parking problem.

Councilman Willis championed the most ambitious improvement of all: the replacement of the worn-out, glass-strewn cinder running track located next to the park at Patrick Henry Junior High School. The track, which enclosed a football field used by four Cleveland public high schools, was both a student and a community resource. (In off hours, residents walked or ran laps around it, having climbed through a large hole in the fenced perimeter to gain access.) Tapping into community development block grants, Willis contributed $250,000 toward the construction of a new $325,000, all-weather, rubberized track. ParkWorks spear-

Sunday in the park. The Greater Friendship Baptist Church has hosted two outdoor worship services that attracted one thousand participants.

headed the effort to raise the additional funds, which came from the Renner Foundation, the Cleveland office of The Trust for Public Land, and some financial legerdemain; it also supervised the construction. A condition of Councilman Willis's support was that the Cleveland Board of Education install a turnstile to allow the community formal and safe access to this much-loved facility.

A newly formed partnership with the Local Initiatives Support Corporation (LISC) led to an unanticipated opportunity to make improvements to the football field at Patrick Henry school as well. Learning about the new Community Fields grant program jointly launched by LISC and the National Football League (NFL), ParkWorks executive director Ann Zoller refused to take no for an answer when told that the grant monies could not be spent on public school facilities. (The NFL feared that it might possibly violate National College Athletic Association recruiting guidelines if it were to invest in selected public school facilities.) Zoller's counterargument proved persuasive. She pointed out that the field and track functioned more as a community resource than as a school asset and suggested that ParkWorks, rather than the Cleveland Municipal School District, serve as project manager and fiscal agent. The NFL subsequently donated $60,000 for reseeding the field and outfitting it with new bleachers and security lighting.

Programmed to Succeed

Smokin'. At the new rubberized, all-weather track at Patrick Henry Junior High School adjoining the park, neighborhood residents join students in pounding out the laps.

Always a staunch ally of Forest Hills Park, Councilman Willis was invited to be the keynote speaker at the community vigil in 2000. He encouraged the families in the audience to patronize the park on a regular basis. "You cannot use a park too much if you're using it for the right things," Willis stated. "You're doing the community a real service by your presence tonight. I'm so pleased to see Forest Hills getting a lot more respect and use." Gesturing toward the nearby police officers, the councilman added: "And I'm especially pleased to say that we haven't yet this year had to call the Sixth District out to deal with an incident in this park."

Indicating that even better days were ahead, Willis shared his commitment to a continuing program of improvements, specifically mentioning new swings and a hiking and biking path that will run the length of the park. The councilman revealed that he was thinking ahead to Phase II, in which the Forest Hills Park bike path would be extended to Lake Erie. Such an extension would link his constituents, via planned expansions of the Cleveland lakefront bikeway and the Towpath Trail, to the recreational and cultural assets of the Cleveland Lakefront State Park, the Cuyahoga Valley National Park, and CanalWay Ohio.

"What do you say we call the bike path 'Mandela Way?'" Willis proposed, eliciting a round of applause.

While future improvements will certainly be welcomed and enjoyed, the citizens of

Come fly with me. An annual Make-a-Kite Clinic has become one of Forest Hills Park's most popular new programs.

Glenville are clearly satisfied with the changes that have already taken place in their community park.

After Willis finished his remarks, a middle-aged man wearing a janitor's uniform, who had dropped by the vigil on his way home from work, came over to look at the Health Walk display. He paused in front of an easel bearing a poster with the headline: "I Like Glenville because . . . ." The display's attendants encouraged the man to finish the sentence by jotting down his thoughts on a lime green sticker to be attached to the poster, which was already dotted with others' sentiments. The man demurred, saying that he did not write very well, but the women insisted. When he completed his labor, one of the women attached his sticker to the poster with a flourish.

"I like Glenville . . . ," the man had written, "because they keep the park clean."

Programmed to Succeed

CLEVELAND LAKEFRONT
STATE PARK

Back in the Swim

CUYAHOGA COUNTY

Every year ten million people visit the Cleveland Lakefront State Park, a chain of six green spaces stretching from the city's far West Side to its border with Euclid on the east. An almost primal desire to get close to the ocean that is Lake Erie helps explain why this is the third busiest state-run park in America.

Even in the dead of winter the parking lots at Edgewater, Gordon, Euclid Beach, Villa Angela, and Wildwood Parks and at the East 55th Street Marina are sprinkled with cars. The occupants are gazing at the icebound lake, fascinated by the stillness and infinite variety of its frozen surfaces. And on weekends from June through September, the parks teem with water worshipers.

West Siders of all ages jam Edgewater's nine-hundred-foot-long swimming beach, as they have done every summer since 1894, when the Cleveland parks commission purchased the land from railroad scion J. B. Perkins. Small-craft owners line up to use six free boat-launch ramps at Gordon Park, the former estate of William J. Gordon. (A wealthy and respected businessman, Gordon in 1892 bequeathed the 122-acre property between East 79th Street and Martin Luther King, Jr., Boulevard to the city for use as a public park.) In the dappled groves at Euclid Beach, a former amusement park near East 156th Street and Lake

Heads above the rest. Cleveland's chain of six lakefront parks satisfies an almost primal desire to get close to the ocean that is Lake Erie. Only two other state-run parks in America attract more visitors.

Shore Boulevard that the state acquired in 1982, picnickers occupy every table. Hot dogs just taste better when eaten at a spot overlooking the lake. Villa Angela—the newest of the state park's units, home to Catholic girls' and boys' schools before its acquisition in 1991—attracts both promenaders and more serious walkers to trails leading through a nature preserve to a scenic boardwalk jutting out over the lake. On breezy days the spray tickles; the views of sunsets are unparalleled.

Villa Angela abuts Wildwood Park, which is located at Neff Road and Lake Shore Boulevard. This one-time beach resort was famous during the Roaring Twenties for its dance hall, admission to which was three cents. The Depression having wreaked havoc on the resort business, the city of Cleveland utilities department bought the lakefront property in the summer of 1938, with the intention of building an intake tunnel for a nearby water filtration plant on the site. Fortunately for the one hundred thousand people then living in Cleveland's Nottingham and Collinwood neighborhoods, who had limited access to the lake, a city councilman threatened to lead a thousand children and a thirty-piece brass band on a protest march if the utilities department failed to immediately open the Wildwood Park beach to the public. Within ten days the beach had been cleaned and opened, establishing a lasting precedent that the land around the mouth of Euclid Creek should be set aside for the enjoyment of East Side Clevelanders.

The water's fine. West Siders of all ages have jammed Edgewater's nine-hundred-foot-long beach every summer since the park opened in 1894.

One Saturday morning in late August 2000 a volunteer Big Sister and her two Little Sisters, Jacquie and Lakeesha, are among the throngs soaking up the seaside-like atmosphere of Cleveland's fifteen-mile-long lakefront. They have come out to Wildwood Park to go canoeing on Euclid Creek. Neither of the teenagers has ever been on a canoeing expedition, and they are giddy with anticipation. As the aluminum canoes are being unloaded from a van, the two girls gleefully splash in the shallows of the creek, chasing after minnows and crayfish with small nets supplied by the state park naturalist. "Watch out for piranhas," the maintenance worker who brought the canoes jokes before departing.

Although Big and Little Sisters listen intently to the naturalist's how-to on paddling, their inexperience shows. They have trouble steering their canoe and are soon going around in circles. "Here we go loop-de-loop," they sing, undaunted, "here we go loop-de-li." Despite

Here we go loop-de-loop. State park naturalist Nora Mercurio attempts to straighten out two inexperienced canoeists during an expedition down Euclid Creek to the lake.

their lack of forward progress, the trio is having a great time. Who wouldn't? Simply being out on the water on a beautiful day is satisfaction enough.

One suspects this sentiment is shared by the dozens of anglers whom the canoeists pass on their half-mile journey up Euclid Creek to Lake Erie. The fisherfolk include two young women, an older female, and a little girl who has been brought out to the Wildwood Park breakwater by her father. She is dressed head to toe in fashionable pink. It has never been easier for those who want to try their hand at sports fishing to gain access to the lake. There's no need to dirty one's clothes or skin one's knee attempting to cross the jagged rocks of a breakwater, now that the Ohio Department of Natural Resources (ODNR) has invested millions in the lakefront parks on new or improved fishing platforms and piers, as well as on building access paths to breakwaters. Still, once safely arrived at the perfect spot, people find that shore fishing is mostly a waiting game.

"You seen any big ones?" a man casting from the bank of Euclid Creek calls out to the passing canoeists. Having spotted only a couple of car tires and a shopping cart in the water, they shake their heads and inquire as to the object of his desire. Steelhead, the fisherman responds, referring to a species of trout that ODNR has been stocking in area rivers that empty into the lake. "They've caught eight of them here," he notes optimistically, "in the last two weeks."

Back in the Swim

Kingfisher territory. Bird watchers make a sighting along Euclid Creek in Wildwood Park.

While experts say that it is possible to catch sports fish such as steelhead, coho salmon, walleye, yellow perch, white bass, and channel catfish from shore, that should not be the exclusive goal of a fishing excursion to the Cleveland Lakefront State Park. "Think of the fish as a bonus," advises Andrew Emrisko, who moors his charter boat, the *Wave Walker,* at the state park's East 55th Street Marina. "You go fishing to relax, enjoy the sun, talk to new people, or spend time with your friends. If God lets you catch a couple of fish, be thankful."

It was not always thus. Early settlers of the Western Reserve had merely to draw a seine net across the mouth of a stream that emptied into the lake, such as Rocky River or Euclid Creek. A wagonload of fish could be hauled in within an hour. Sturgeon were so plentiful (and big!—some topped seven feet) that they became a staple of free lunch counters at every turn-of-the-century saloon between Toledo and Buffalo. Indeed, before untreated wastewater discharges, agricultural runoff, and industrial pollution contaminated its waters; before urban development destroyed its wetland spawning grounds and zebra mussels and round gobies disrupted its food chain, Lake Erie was considered the most productive body of fresh water *in the world.* Commercial catches at their height between 1913 and 1925 averaged 58 million pounds annually. But overexploitation was beginning to take its toll on the lake's populations of whitefish, herring, sturgeon, pike, pickerel, bass, walleye, and perch. By the early 1950s catches had dwindled to under 20 million pounds annually. Yet even then Lake Erie re-

Gone fishin'. Recreational usage leaped after the state of Ohio took over management of Cleveland's decaying lakefront parks in 1978 and poured millions into their rehabilitation.

mained an angler's paradise. Andrew Emrisko, who has been fishing in the lake for nearly fifty years, remembers the days when "you could catch perch by the bucket off the shore" at the lakefront parks. "From April to October guys were elbow to elbow on the rocks."

Sports fishing became more of a challenge in a lake whose waters had turned pea green and murky by the late 1960s. In 1970 a high level of mercury attributable to industrial contaminants shut down commercial fishing in Lake Erie for a year. Alarmed by algae blooms, a rash of closed beaches, and toxic fish, the Great Lakes states subsequently spent billions on the construction of wastewater treatment plants. Although this and other environmental initiatives have markedly improved Lake Erie's clarity and purity, mercury levels remain sufficiently high today to merit a state advisory against the consumption of more than one meal of lake fish per week by women of childbearing age and by children under six.

As the lake appeared to be dying, neglect of Cleveland's municipal green spaces took the fun out of visiting even the lakefront parks. Mayoral administrations, increasingly strapped for operating funds, allowed recreational facilities to run down or close. Illegal dumping and vandalism added to the disreputable appearance of Edgewater, Gordon, and Wildwood Parks, much to the dismay of their patrons and supporters. One of them, Cleveland landscape architect William A. Behnke, decided to take action.

Behnke, who had enjoyed swimming at Gordon Park as a boy, began to speak to various community groups about the "tragic state of disrepair" of Cleveland's once nationally regarded park system. In response, the Shaker Lakes Garden Center and The Cleveland Foundation commissioned William A. Behnke Associates to document the problem and recommend solutions. Behnke's *Cleveland Parks and Recreation Study,* released in 1974 under the auspices of the Growth Association of Greater Cleveland, became the means by which Cleveland city planning director Norman Krumholz persuaded Republican mayor Ralph J. Perk that something must be done to reverse the consequences of the administration's 40 percent reduction of the parks budget. The mayor convened a seven-member Lakefront Task Force to determine how to improve maintenance at Edgewater and Gordon Parks.

In the wake of Hurricane Agnes in 1973, Krumholz had already suggested to Cleveland City Council that the lakefront parks be placed under the auspices of a broader taxing authority with the means of repairing damages caused by the high winds. Now task force member Thomas F. Patton—a retired steel industry executive and Cleveland Foundation trustee with close ties to then Ohio governor James A. Rhodes—paid a visit to the governor's mansion for the sole purpose of persuading his fellow Republican that responsibility for the lakefront parks should be transferred from the city to the state.

Rhodes, who was then running in what would be a losing race against Democrat Richard F. Celeste, may have okayed the idea as a means of gaining support in Cuyahoga County. For his part, Mayor Perk had nothing to lose by relinquishing management of the lakefront parks, as he was on his way out of office, having been defeated by Dennis Kucinich. In early 1978, as one of his last acts, Perk signed documents authorizing the state of Ohio's lease of Edgewater, Gordon, and Wildwood Parks for a period of fifty years. At the time of the lease agreement there was not a single working toilet in any of the three parks!

Within a year the Ohio Department of Natural Resources spent $7 million to fix the comfort stations, clean up the illegal dumping sites, enhance security, and construct new facilities in the lakefront parks. Three new fishing platforms at Gordon Park were among the first capital improvements, as ODNR sought to respond to needs identified by Cleveland's city council members.

Recognizing that the state park system was unfamiliar with the complexities of managing urban waterfront parks, The Cleveland Foundation obtained a grant from the German Marshall Fund to send ODNR's director, a state representative from Cleveland who sat on the budget committee of the Ohio House, and Bill Behnke (among others) to tour mixed-use waterfronts in fourteen European cities. The contingent saw how green spaces, retail shops, restaurants, and housing add vibrancy to shipping and industry districts. Once somewhat leery of ODNR's added responsibility, the government officials came back excited about the recreational potential of the new state parks. Over the next decade the Ohio Assembly approved a total of $40 million in capital appropriations for the Cleveland Lakefront State Park, ensuring not only that its properties would be well maintained and safe, but that they would blossom with new marinas, boat launches, fishing piers, hike and bike paths, and picnic areas. As charter boat captain Andrew Emrisko, a close observer of the transformation, puts it: "The state has improved the parks 2,000 percent."

The parks' proponents even filled a longstanding void in the recreational amenities available to East Side Clevelanders: a scarcity of public swimming beaches. In 1982, the City of Cleveland, responding to a recommendation from the Cleveland office of the Trust for Public Land, purchased a sixteen-acre waterfront parcel from the owners of the old Euclid Beach amusement park and turned it over to ODNR. (The Cleveland Foundation and other local philanthropies matched the monies the city mustered for the acquisition.) Leaders of this public-private partnership joined hands again in 1985 to purchase thirty acres of waterfront property behind the recently closed Villa Angela Academy, an acquisition that opened up another large swimming beach for public enjoyment. Two years later, ODNR purchased a small parcel at the rear of the Euclid Beach trailer park, forging the final link in a continuous strip of Lake Erie shoreline accessible to the public, from Euclid Beach Park to Wildwood Park. In a state that has lost 85 percent of its lakefront to private development, this was truly a priceless initiative.

Through several changes of political leadership, the state of Ohio's commitment to the lakefront parks has remained unwavering. In 2000, for example, Edgewater Park received $2.7 million for renovations, its biggest facelift since the transfer of ownership. Under ODNR regional park manager Wayne A. Holmes, operating monies have been found to add a naturalist to the staff, making it possible for the lakefront parks to offer educational programming and guided activities (such as Wildwood Park's Saturday-morning canoe trips) for the first time.

It is only fitting that Lake Erie—Ohio's most popular recreational destination, as well as

Unparalleled. The stunning view from the Gordon Park breakwater attracts visitors at all hours of the day.

its most precious natural resource—should once again have a platinum setting. Reflecting on what the lake has contributed to the quality of life in this region, the Sierra Club's Great Lakes specialist Glenn Landers notes: "It has defined our industry and provided a means of transporting of our goods. It determines our weather and, in the summertime at least, it dominates our recreation. We *are* Lake Erie, and we should do everything we can to preserve it for everyone's enjoyment."

Jacquie and Lakeesha would certainly agree, having finally reached that seeming ocean of water on their canoe expedition. Realizing that the teenagers would never get beyond the first bend in Euclid Creek if she did not take over the chore of steering, state park naturalist Nora Mercurio volunteered to replace their Big Sister and paddled the girls' canoe up to the mouth of the creek. The teenagers came back from their venture onto the lake's slightly choppy waters as exhilarated as if they had been on a killer roller coaster. "Can we do this again next year?" Jacquie begged her Big Sister. "It was too much fun!"

ROCKEFELLER PARK

The Value of Networking

CLEVELAND

The first thing you notice when you take a ride through Rockefeller Park are the flowers. Huge masses of blossoms dot the roadside and glens throughout the warm months of the year—daffodils in the spring, day lilies in the early summer, and black-eyed Susans in early

On new footing. An annual distribution of funds from the Holden Trust has made it possible for the city of Cleveland to improve the ambience and amenities of Rockefeller Park. As a result, people are reconnecting with this historic green space.

Signs of change. Massive plantings of colorful flowers have replaced the refuse that used to litter the hillsides in Rockefeller Park.

fall. The grass is neatly trimmed, the invasive vegetation that once lined Doan Brook has been pruned back, and the refuse that always seemed to litter the hillsides for most of the last twenty-five years is gone. Benches now boast all of their slats, and security lighting has been installed in strategic locations.

Even the area around the Wade Park Avenue Lagoon has been restored to its proper place as the historic heart of Rockefeller Park. The lagoon, known to turn-of-the-century Clevelanders as Brewery Pond (a beer manufacturer then overlooked the water from a nearby hilltop), served as a fishing hole and ice-skating rink into the 1950s. Subsequent city administrations had allowed the lagoon (not to be confused with the similarly named reflecting pond in front of the nearby Cleveland Museum of Art) slowly to become a swamp, but it has now been dredged, and repaved pathways encircle the water. A parking lot has been constructed nearby, providing easy access both to the lagoon and to a new play area equipped with a bright blue and green jungle gym. Plans call for adding a shelter house to the lagoon's attractions.

In short, Rockefeller Park is no longer the "neglected, vandalized jungle of overgrowth, ill-lighted, polluted and unsafe" that the *Cleveland Press* described in 1981. That year marked the beginning of the park's comeback, for it saw the publication of an influential study that sounded the alarm about Rockefeller Park's deterioration. The study, prepared by the Cleveland landscape architecture firm of William A. Behnke & Associates with the support

The heart of the park. Once popular as an ice-skating rink and fishing hole but eventually allowed to become a swamp, the Wade Avenue Lagoon has been restored to its historic preeminence.

of The Cleveland Foundation, outlined a master plan for the park's restoration. Lack of resources kept the plan on the shelf until 1990, when Rockefeller Park became the beneficiary of an annual distribution from the Holden Trust, which had come into being in 1988 according to the wishes of Albert Fairchild Holden, an heir to the *Cleveland Plain Dealer* publishing fortune. Holden's will specified that life trusts established for his daughters should, upon their demise, provide annual income for either the Holden Arboretum or, if the Arboretum was financially secure, Rockefeller Park. At the request of the trust administrators, Behnke Associates updated the original master plan. This document, which was again updated in 1995 and 2000, has guided the expenditure of the trust's yearly distribution of $250,000 to Rockefeller Park. To date, the Holden Trust seed money has leveraged approximately $10 million in capital improvements recommended and designed by Behnke Associates. Tom Zarfoss, a principal of the firm, has served as project manager, working closely with city and trust officials to effect Rockefeller's astounding transformation.

The most important change of all? People are reconnecting with the park. Playing tennis. Chatting on its benches. Lazing alongside the banks of Doan Brook. Fishing in the lagoon. Rolling head over heels with their friends down its grassy slopes. Or just cruising along, hair ruffling in the breeze.

It's nice to see the return of that particular pastime. Clevelanders have been suggesting,

Doan Brook. To counter the perception that the park was unsafe, overgrown vegetation was cut back, opening up the view and the accessibility of the meandering stream.

"Let's go for a ride in Rockefeller Park," ever since its creation in the 1890s. During that decade a newly created parks commission with the power to issue bonds established Cleveland's great municipal parks. In addition to Rockefeller Park, these included Edgewater, Brookside, Garfield, Washington, and Shaker Lakes. The nucleus of Rockefeller Park was assembled in 1893, when the parks commission, acting on the recommendation put forth in the Cleveland Park Plan that "outlying parks could be readily united and connected by a broad smoothly paved boulevard, enclosing the city," purchased two hundred separate parcels in the Doan Brook Valley on Cleveland's far East Side. The commissioners intended to build a parkway through this property that would connect two tracts of parkland donated to the city by telegraph industry leader Jeptha H. Wade and iron-ore broker William J. Gordon.

Even granting that the city had been starved for green space until this time, it is almost impossible to conceive of the immense popularity of the Eastern Parkway that was subsequently built. Try picturing this. On a warm Sunday in May 1896, someone decided to count the people who came to take in the spring air and the scenery in Rockefeller Park as they passed back and forth on the parkway between Wade Park in what is now University Circle and Gordon Park on the shores of Lake Erie. At the end of the day the tally stood at 43,715 passersby. The breakdown, according to mode of transportation, was 14,873 gentlefolk in carriages, 14,690 people on bicycles, and 14,152 pedestrians.

Rockefeller Park

Hanging out. The return of people—to play, chat, or relax—has been the most important of all the changes evident in the park.

The coming of the automobile did little to diminish recreational use of the Eastern Parkway, which by then had been extended up into the Heights as far as the Shaker Lakes, using $300,000 that had been presented to the city by Standard Oil Company founder John D. Rockefeller on the occasion of Cleveland's centennial. Rockefeller stipulated that the monies must be used to improve and beautify the parklands that now bear his name, which he also presented to the city in 1896. This land, some 276 acres straddling the Eastern Parkway, was valued at $600,000. The industrialist later contributed another $100,000 to underwrite the architectural embellishment of four monumental Romanesque bridges that were built over the Eastern Parkway between 1898 and 1900 to divert traffic on Wade Park, Superior, and St. Clair Avenues, and to elevate a lakeshore railroad line. The work of Cleveland architect Charles F. Schweinfurth (the designer of Trinity Cathedral, the Union Club, and Harkness Chapel on the Case Western Reserve University campus), the bridges are "among the most pleasing ornaments in Cleveland's landscape," according to Eric Johannesen's history of the city's architecture. They became sufficient reason in themselves to visit Rockefeller Park.

Within a quarter of a century, the parkway had gained such a prominent place in the life of the city that it was chosen as the location for a moving tribute to Cleveland's World War I dead. For every serviceman who fell in combat, an oak tree was planted along the parkway.

Room for everyone. In celebration of Cleveland's centennial, Standard Oil Company founder John D. Rockefeller gave the city 276 acres of land straddling Doan Brook for use as a public park.

At the foot of each tree a round bronze plaque bore the name of the serviceman it honored. On Memorial Day 1919, when "Liberty Row" was unveiled, the dimension of the city's loss became poignantly clear. Liberty Row stretched from the lakefront up into Shaker Heights. Today only a few plaques remain (most notably, along North Park Boulevard in Cleveland Heights). Even so, one can easily imagine the emotional impact of a Sunday drive in those days on the parkway, which was renamed Liberty Boulevard. It must have been similar to that experienced today at the Vietnam Veterans Memorial in Washington, D.C.

With the construction in the 1950s of an interchange connecting the new Memorial Shoreway to Liberty Boulevard, the automobile finally made its presence felt in Rockefeller Park. Often traveling at high speed, cars carrying commuters pushed "Sunday drivers" off the parkway. During the city's slide toward default in 1978, deferred maintenance of park facilities and grounds discouraged patronage, as well. Incidents of hoodlums dropping concrete blocks off the Schweinfurth bridges onto the windshields of passing cars confirmed the public perception that it was not safe to venture into Rockefeller Park.

Liberty Boulevard was renamed Martin Luther King, Jr., Boulevard in 1981. It remains a busy commuter route to this day. However, thanks to the efforts of former Cleveland mayor Michael R. White, it is once again possible to traverse Rockefeller Park in safety and at one's leisure, traveling on foot, on roller blades, or by bike.

Rockefeller Park

"Pleasing ornaments." Four monumental Romanesque bridges built between 1898 and 1900 span Rockefeller Park's main drive. The work of famed Cleveland architect Charles F. Schweinfurth, they are reason enough to visit.

During White's second term, which began in 1994, his administration won funding from the federal government and the Ohio Department of Transportation to construct an asphalt bike trail in the park that would run down both sides of MLK Boulevard from Wade Lagoon to the lakefront. A recommendation of the Behnke master plan, the bike path was completed in summer 1997 at a cost of $650,000 and named in honor of the Cleveland track star Harrison Dillard, a four-time Olympic gold medalist. It feeds right into the Cleveland lake front bikeway (a concept also proposed by Behnke Associates as part of the firm's 1979 master plan for the Cleveland Lakefront State Park). At present, the lakefront bikeway runs along Lake Shore Boulevard from Euclid Beach Park to Gordon Park, then extends along North Marginal Road to East Ninth Street downtown. A planned western extension will lead bicyclists over to Edgewater Park and on to the city's western border.

Civic and government leaders in Cleveland's near eastern suburbs are already informally discussing a network of bike trails that could conceivably converge at the Shaker Lakes, where they would connect with an existing bike path built by the city of Cleveland Heights along North Park Boulevard. Cost and logistics aside, it is easy to conceive of an extension of the Cleveland Heights bike path that would connect with the Harrison Dillard Bikeway in Rockefeller Park. If the Towpath Trail is also extended—south from Akron to New Philadelphia and north from Cleveland's East 49th Street to the Flats, as has been proposed by

The Value of Networking

Welcome attention. During the mayoral administration of Michael R. White, who played in the park as a boy, the city made a concerted effort to improve maintenance and safety.

the Ohio & Erie Canal Management Plan of 2000—bicyclists will be able to pedal through Rockefeller and Edgewater Parks on dedicated paths to the lakefront from their homes on Cleveland's East and West Sides or in its bordering suburbs. They could then bike along Lake Erie on designated routes into downtown Cleveland and take the off-street Towpath Trail through the Cuyahoga River Valley to Akron and on into central Ohio. Really big thinkers are dreaming of extending the Cleveland Lakefront Bikeway, into which the Towpath Trail would feed, all the way to the state borders: Toledo on the west and Conneaut on the east. Interconnectivity is the holy grail of regional park planners and the hallmark of an excellent regional parks network.

White freely confesses to having a personal connection to Rockefeller Park. He played there as a child and still lives near it. Under his watch, the city made a concerted effort to improve the park's maintenance and safety. The White administration also secured a pool of monies for capital improvements by bringing legal action against the Holden Trust, which named the park as a secondary beneficiary. The city won its argument that the park was as deserving as the primary beneficiary: Holden Arboretum. Two seats on the five-member Holden Trust distribution committee are now held by political appointees, giving the city of Cleveland a hand in determining how the trust's funds are spent in Rockefeller Park.

"It is gratifying to see the positive changes," observes former distribution committee

The new Harrison Dillard Bikeway. Named in honor of the Cleveland track star and four-time Olympic gold medalist, a bike path that runs the length of the park and feeds into the lakefront bikeway was completed in the summer of 1997.

chairperson C. W. Eliot Payne. "We're thrilled that we have been able to help the city restore this beautiful gateway into University Circle."

For more and more Clevelanders, the park is once again an attractive destination in and of itself. One warm Saturday evening not too long ago a father and two daughters could be seen riding their bicycles through the park on the Harrison Dillard Bikeway. The family obviously regarded the outing as a special occasion. Not only were the little girls dressed in their Sunday-best play clothes, but dad looked spiffy, too. Having come full circle, Rockefeller Park is once again a popular place to connect with the action, to see and be seen.

CLEVELAND
CULTURAL GARDENS

A Place to Remember, Part Two

ROCKEFELLER PARK, UNIVERSITY CIRCLE

September 19, 1999, was a big day for the Carpatho-Rusyns of Greater Cleveland. That Sunday, a ceremony organized by members of this tiny Slavic ethnic group, indigenous to the Carpathian Mountain region of East Central Europe, was to be the center of attention at

The Hungarian Garden. Twenty-five different ethnic groups have built landscaped sculpture courts in Rockefeller Garden to commemorate the national heroes, artists, and philosophers of their countries of origin.

One World Day. Folk dancers from Cleveland's Italian American community participate in a day-long celebration of their cultural heritage that has taken place annually in Rockefeller Park for more than fifty years.

Cleveland's One World Day festival. At around two o'clock that afternoon, with then Mayor Michael R. White looking on, leaders of the local Rusyn American community intended to return a bust of a Rusyn patriot to its rightful place in the Rusin Garden* in Rockefeller Park.

In 1958, the original likeness of Eastern Orthodox priest Alexander Duchnovich had disappeared from the collection of statuary and monuments in the park's Cultural Gardens, a series of landscaped sculpture courts that commemorate the contributions to world culture made by the national heroes, artists, and philosophers of twenty-five different ethnic groups. The majority of the cultural gardens were built between the two world wars by some of the nationality groups making up the larger mosaic of Cleveland. In 1939 the Rusin Garden became the thirteenth member of the ensemble, joining Eastern European gardens already contributed by the city's Polish, Yugoslav, Czech, and Slovak communities.

Seeking an appropriate way to celebrate the Rusin Garden's sixtieth anniversary in 1999, the Rusyn American community of Greater Cleveland had deemed it fitting to commission a replacement bust of Alexander Duchnovich, whom the Rusyns revere as their George Washington. A nationless people, the Carpatho-Rusyns have lived under the rule of Austria-Hungary, Czechoslovakia, the Soviet Union, and the Ukraine. Duchnovich, a priest with

---

*Rusin was the preferred spelling at the time of the garden's creation.

the heart of a poet and historian, helped to give his people a sense of identity through his authorship of a national anthem and a Rusyn prayer book.

The Rusin Garden, where the unveiling of the bust was to take place, is situated in the oldest section of the Cleveland Cultural Gardens, a strand of eighteen sculpture courts extending along East Boulevard between Superior and St. Clair Avenues. In 1927 this section of Rockefeller Park was set aside by Cleveland City Council for what the enabling legislation called a "Poet's Corner." In truth, the leading proponent of the Cultural Gardens had a much more compelling monument in mind.

Jewish Independent newspaper editor and publisher Leo Weidenthal took his inspiration from the Shakespeare Garden, a splendid English glade that had been established in Rockefeller Park in 1916 to mark the tercentenary of that towering playwright's death. Using plantings associated with Shakespeare or his plays, such as cuttings from a mulberry tree planted by the dramatist himself in Stratford, sycamore maples transplanted from Scotland's Birnam Wood, and roses from the grave of the young woman presumed to be the real-life Juliet and donated to Cleveland by the mayor of Verona, Italy, the city parks department created an Elizabethan setting for a commemorative bust of the Bard. Weidenthal successfully propagated the idea that the city of Cleveland should encourage all of its nationality groups to enshrine their cultural giants in Rockefeller Park, thus creating a panorama of world culture that would forever stir souls as a symbol of international unity and good will.

Perhaps because of the homogenization of American life, the symbolism of the Cleveland Cultural Gardens has lost some of its comprehensibility and power over time. The 1970s witnessed the last flurry of planning for new gardens, and several of these, such as the African American Garden, the Native American Garden, and the Indian Garden, have still to be fully realized. The completion of a Chinese garden in the 1990s near Wade Park was made possible by a boost from the Taiwanese government. The gardens' commemorative function has also been diminished by the theft or vandalism of a number of its sixty original commemorative bronze busts and plaques. (Alas, even the monumental head of Will Shakespeare has been spirited away from its place of honor in what is now known as the British Garden.) Yet the refinement of the landscape architecture endures.

The gardens along East Boulevard, artfully unified by a series of winding paths and stairways designed in 1936 by the city's newly created division of landscape architecture (and

A wedding ceremony in the Greek Garden. For some the Cultural Gardens are a symbol of international unity; others are entranced by their beauty.

recently restored as part of a larger capital improvement campaign in Rockefeller Park), are at once harmonious and charmingly individual. Each has a distinctive personality. An elaborate wrought-iron gateway beckons at the entrance to the Hungarian Garden. A sunken patio framed by twin Doric columns and terraced beds of fragrant lavender is the hidden heart of the Greek Garden. The Irish Garden traces the form of a Celtic cross; the Hebrew Garden, a six-pointed star. A heroic bronze statue of Goethe and Schiller standing arm in arm dominates the central *Platz* of the German Garden.

Some of the sculpture courts along East Boulevard derive considerable dramatic effect from their elevated position on a wooded hillside above Doan Brook. The upper esplanade of the Italian Garden expands into a balustraded overlook in whose center rises a magnificent (if inoperative) marble-bowl fountain. From such a romantic setting one would not be surprised to enjoy a vista of Tuscan hills. In the imposing Lithuanian Garden, twin staircases spill over the hillside like mighty rivers of stone. The Rusin Garden, on the other hand, makes a virtue of simplicity. Its small upper tier, entered off East Boulevard near Superior Avenue, consists of an unadorned sandstone plaza bordered by low hedges. A narrow stone stairway winds from the upper terrace down a steep slope to a wooded glen that shelters a large sandstone terrace. This plaza is capped by an elevated semicircular stone stage on which sits Duchnovich's plinth. The plinth is headless.

The Rusin Garden. Many of the sixty bronze busts and plaques originally placed throughout the gardens have been spirited away, including the bust of Rusyn priest, poet, and historian Alexander Duchnovich that once graced this plinth.

The spiritual leaders of the Byzantine Catholic Eparchy of Parma, Ohio, who commissioned the replacement bust, determined that it was best to take the sculpture back with them to that Cleveland suburb at the conclusion of One World Day. "We would like to leave it in the park," one of the religious leaders confessed to the hundred or so persons who witnessed the bust's unveiling. "But I spent thirty-one years looking for the last one."

The public's perceptions are hard to change. Yet the Cleveland Cultural Gardens have clearly rebounded from the days when, not so long ago, they justified their description by a *Plain Dealer* reporter as a "no-man's land." The scars of decay, litter, and graffiti have largely been erased. This comeback has been the work of many hands. Mini-grants from the Holden Trust, which expends some $250,000 a year on improvements to Rockefeller Park, have made it possible for the sponsoring communities to assess the nature and cost of repairs needed to ensure the structural stability of each garden. The Rockefeller Parks Cultural Arts Association has attempted to bring people back into the gardens and the park by organizing events and programs, and the Cleveland Cultural Garden Federation, an umbrella oversight organization, persists in its attempt to cultivate a renewed sense of ownership among the sponsoring communities.

Thanks to the recruitment efforts of past federation presidents Alfonso D'Emilia and Richard Konisiewicz, a number of gardens enjoy the ministrations of a small band of loy-

A no-man's-land no longer. Thanks to the efforts of loyal volunteer gardeners and caretakers, the litter and graffiti that once scarred the gardens have largely been erased.

alists willing to undertake cleanup and flower-planting chores several times a year. An even greater emotional and financial investment will be needed to ensure the health and beauty of the Cleveland Cultural Gardens for future generations. In a 1997 study, Behnke Associates, the Cleveland landscape architecture firm that is supervising restoration of Rockefeller Park, estimated that it will cost more than $4 million to return the gardens to a close approximation of their original condition. The federation's current president, George P. Parras, hopes to establish a broad-based conservancy similar to the New York City not-for-profit organization that has raised more than $200 million for the restoration of Central Park. Membership would be open to all those interested in helping to preserve the Cleveland Cultural Gardens as a unique national treasure.

Parras has already succeeded in reviving the interest of his fellow Greek Americans, who have relandscaped their garden. He has also persuaded the sponsoring communities to speak with one voice in dealing with the city of Cleveland. In response, the city has awarded the Cleveland Cultural Garden Federation a small grant to prepare a landscape lighting master plan, one of the top priorities identified in a concept paper outlining the role and responsibilities of Parras's proposed conservancy.

Cleveland's relatively small community of Rusyns provides some of the newest recruits to the cause. Members of the Cleveland chapter poured their hearts into their featured appearance at One World Day. Young Rusyn women passed around loaves of bread and salt,

The Irish Garden. Although some sculpture courts are well maintained, fountains and stonework in others have decayed. It will cost upwards of four million dollars to restore all the gardens to their original condition.

a traditional gesture of welcome, while a troop of Rusyn folk dancers, singers, and musicians performed. Before and after the unveiling, festival-goers slowly climbed the stairs to the upper terrace of the Rusin Garden to view a small cultural exhibit. On display were racks of Rusyn peasant costumes and tables bearing Rusyn craft and food items, Carpatho-Rusyn Society literature, and stacks of T-shirts bearing such slogans as "Carpatho-Rusyn and Proud" and "Carpatho-Rusyns Are Everywhere."

The latter slogan hints at the reason for the Rusyns' attachment to the Rusin Garden. Only half a million Rusyns still live in the shadow of the Carpathian Mountains, while approximately 750,000 individuals of Carpatho-Rusyn ancestry are now scattered throughout

The path ahead. The Cleveland Cultural Gardens Federation hopes to establish a broad-based private support group to raise the funds needed to preserve this unique national treasure.

the United States as a result of their parents' and grandparents' uprooting by the tumult of the twentieth century. The Carpatho-Rusyn Society, a national cultural organization based in Pittsburgh with a mission to keep alive the traditions of this country-less people, has taken on the maintenance of the Rusin Garden in Cleveland as an official project. After all, this simple plot is the closest the Rusyns come to having a land they can call their own. One can only hope that their example of renewed stewardship will inspire some of Cleveland's larger, more affluent ethnic groups to reclaim their gardens, as well.

CLEVELAND'S NEW ELEMENTARY SCHOOL PLAYGROUNDS

Springboards for Change

VARIOUS CLEVELAND NEIGHBORHOODS

The dedication of a new playground at George Washington Carver Elementary School in Cleveland's Central neighborhood was an exhilarating occasion even for the adults. Not often do you see a grownup zooming down the twists and turns of a children's slide. Yet on

A dream no longer deferred. A state-of-the-art playground has replaced a barren side yard at George Washington Carver Elementary School in Cleveland, much to the delight of the students, who previously had nowhere to play during recess except a crumbling asphalt parking lot.

Challenging. The "School Grounds as Community Parks" initiative, spearheaded by urban parks advocate ParkWorks, seeks to build new playgrounds and learning gardens at more than eighty of the city's public elementary schools. After the playground was built at Carver, parental and local business involvement at the school jumped.

that particular September day in 1999, there was former Cleveland Browns great Bernie Kosar —all six feet five inches of him—happily negotiating the curves of a helix-shaped slide, one of two in a brightly colored jungle gym that was the centerpiece of the new Carver playground.

The multilevel structure and its companion outdoor science and math learning lab (complete with herb, shade, butterfly, and vegetable gardens) represented the first success in the "School Grounds as Community Parks" initiative of ParkWorks, a not-for-profit urban parks advocacy organization based in Cleveland. As honorary co-chair of the initiative, Kosar was there to help dedicate the new facility, as were Cleveland Municipal School District CEO Barbara Byrd-Bennett, the trustees of ParkWorks, and then Cleveland mayor Michael R. White. Reacting to the joyfulness of the occasion, Kosar, a former National Football League quarterback, decided to inaugurate the equipment in high style.

Springboards for Change

Lessons and larks. While primarily intended to be used as an outdoor science and math learning lab, the learning garden at Carver has become a favorite relaxation spot for students and teachers alike.

After his short trip down the slide, Kosar was quickly overrun by the more than 450 Carver students in attendance, who rushed forward, laughing and shouting, to test the mettle of the new equipment. The Carver kids needed no instruction in how to derive maximum satisfaction from their new playthings, installed on a user-friendly rubberized safety surface. In fact, one youngster—nearly overcome with excitement—executed a series of Olympic-caliber back flips down the length of the cushiony surface just to mark the moment.

A year before, Mayor White had moved on his belief that constructive play opportunities should be a part of every child's educational experience. At the time, that was not always the case in Cleveland. Given the woeful state of many public school play facilities in the city, the mayor had asked ParkWorks to take the lead in a playground-building campaign—a sort of Marshall Plan for the community's struggling public schools. The goal was to provide state-of-the-art playgrounds and outdoor learning gardens at every elementary school in the district that lacked these facilities. The estimated price tag for the entire program was a daunting $20 million.

ParkWorks agreed to undertake a pilot project to develop a model that could be replicated throughout Cleveland. The organization would raise the necessary funding for the pilot facility, establish a design process that would include input from students and the community, and oversee construction. The Cleveland Municipal School District would be responsible for providing ongoing maintenance for the prototype.

Based on a review of neighborhood poverty indices, George Washington Carver Elementary was chosen as the site for the model playground and outdoor learning lab. Located on East 55th Street between Cedar and Central Avenues in the middle of one of Cleveland's most impoverished areas, the institution reflected its surroundings all too well. Carver kids let off excess energy at recess on the school's rutted and crumbling asphalt parking lot or on the sun-baked and featureless moonscape of the side yard. More often than not, they had to invent games that required equipment no more elaborate than a ball.

Similar schoolyard conditions greeted more than forty thousand Cleveland schoolchildren every day. At the time, only seventeen of the city's eighty-two elementary schools boasted adequately equipped play areas. Upgrading or even maintaining schoolgrounds was of necessity a low priority in a financially strapped system that was struggling to reverse decades of academic and physical-plant decline. New roofs, windows, and mechanical systems were just a few of the improvements that were desperately needed at schools throughout the district, so playgrounds were generally perceived as luxuries. Indeed, on the "Top 30" priority list of Carver's principal, a fully equipped new playground had ranked near the bottom.

But ParkWorks executive director Ann Zoller knew what a vibrant playground could do for a school and its surrounding community, having attended an urban parks conference in Chicago, where she had learned about that city's "Campus Park" program. The Chicago initiative, launched in 1995, had been successful in revamping seventy-five school playgrounds. Once students all over the city had safe and enjoyable play areas, teachers reported better classroom behavior and performance from their charges. In addition, the Campus Park program seemed to spur improvements in otherwise downtrodden districts. Many of the seventy-five neighborhoods in which school playgrounds were built reported a surge in new housing and business development and a drop in crime rates and utilization of local hospital emergency rooms.

The Chicago initiative proved that school playgrounds serve a dual role: They are healthy and necessary outlets for the energy of schoolchildren, and they are also essential elements of vibrant city neighborhoods. Good playgrounds engage children in positive ways. They provide spaces for constructive play, as well as for informal education—about social norms,

Constructive play. Former Cleveland mayor Michael R. White launched the playgrounds initiative in 1998, acting on his conviction that every child should have a safe and engaging place to let off steam. As of the summer of 2001, twenty-four new playgrounds had been built in Cleveland neighborhoods. Some new playgrounds have prompted additional community greening efforts.

teamwork, even design and simple physics. Because access to nearby parks and play areas is increasingly important in attracting new home buyers and retaining existing homeowners, playgrounds also renew a city's livability. And they provide a venue for area residents to meet, talk, and get to know one another. In short, a well-designed and well-maintained playground can be the focal point of a neighborhood.

ParkWorks formally launched the School Grounds as Community Parks initiative in the fall of 1998. That season, a benefit party marking the opening of downtown Cleveland's new Hard Rock Café kicked off the fund-raising effort. The benefit raised $30,000, an important first step. ParkWorks raised the remaining $200,000 needed for the Carver pilot from a variety of sources. The potential benefits of the School Grounds project—buttressed by reports detailing the results of the Chicago program—favorably impressed the principals of The 1525 Foundation, the Eva L. and Joseph M. Bruening Foundation, the Harry K. and Emma R. Fox Foundation, the Hershey Family Foundation, the Bernie J. Kosar Charitable Trust, the Gries Family Foundation, the Norcross Wildlife Fund, the Cleveland Cliffs Foundation, Ronald McDonald House Charities, and Mr. and Mrs. Joseph H. Thomas. The gardens of the prototype outdoor learning lab would be donated by Cleveland Botanical Garden, and repaving of Carver's parking lot—to accommodate a running track and basketball courts—would be funded by Cleveland city councilman Frank Jackson.

Just one year after the School Grounds initiative was formulated, George Washington Carver Elementary's beautiful new playground facility was dedicated. Carver kids immediately began to enjoy every aspect of the play and learning areas. Carver teachers became the envy of their peers, as they conducted lessons outdoors and held meetings amidst the flowers and trees of the learning garden. Even more important, parental interaction with the school quickly increased. And nearby businesses and institutions began to seek out Carver's principal to ask how they, too, could get involved.

Neighborhood involvement is a recurring theme in discussions of new parks and playgrounds. The absence of attractive open spaces can have a powerful negative effect on an area—an effect that even the smallest green space can help to ameliorate. And concerned residents can make all the difference in laying the groundwork for the creation of these kinds of resources.

A case in point is the example set by Mark McGraw, a tavern owner in Cleveland's North Collinwood neighborhood. McGraw understood that healthy neighborhood schools were essential to healthy neighborhoods, and that both were essential to a healthy business climate. But he was also personally affected by the condition of nearby Oliver Hazard Perry Elementary School, where his late mother had been a pupil many years before.

Passing the institution several times each day on errands for his business, McGraw eventually decided that the Perry kids deserved something better than the school's barren, joyless landscape. One day in 1998, he decided to drop by the school and discuss his interest in a new playground with the principal, Jane Petschauer.

That visit would set in motion a remarkable series of events. Within weeks, a group of

How does your garden grow? Carver's learning garden, which was donated by Cleveland Botanical Garden, is divided into sections devoted to herbs, butterfly-attracting and shade plants, and vegetables. Though compact, the design affords students a comprehensive introduction to the many uses of plants.

involved Perry parents was working with McGraw to develop a campaign to raise $150,000 for a new playground for the Perry school. The campaign would eventually include Wednesday "Burger Nites" at McGraw's Time Out Grille, from which he would donate fifty cents to the playground project for every hamburger purchased. McGraw sold instant bingo tickets to his customers, with proceeds going to the playground fund. The parents' committee held two elaborate fund-raisers, both of which were catered—for free—by the Time Out Grille. And after six months, a major commitment of support was secured from Cleveland City Council president Michael Polensek.

Less than a year after McGraw's first visit to the Perry school, more than $150,000 had been raised and invested in two new playground areas—one designed for the school's older students, the other for younger kids from the school and the neighborhood. And planning was already underway for a third playground, as well as for a commemorative plaza.

As McGraw's story so clearly illustrates, ordinary people will take extraordinary measures to support projects that result in parks and play spaces for their communities. The appeal may be purely economic: the rise in property values that generally occurs in the vicinity of new park facilities. Or it may be emotional: the memory of one's own happy childhood days, or the desire to see new generations of children enjoy simple outdoor pleasures. But whatever the reason, the opportunity to embellish our communities with parks, playgrounds, or other green spaces seems to call up the best in all of us.

No wonder, then, that during its first construction season, ParkWorks found sufficient support to complete three state-of-the-art schoolground parks, plus an additional five financed by Cleveland City Council. The following year, nearly double that number of projects was completed. Early challenge grants from local foundations had leveraged more than $5 million in funding for the initiative, covering the costs of construction for twenty-four school playgrounds in neighborhoods with poverty rates greater than 50 percent.

Based on the response from residents of areas in which new playground/parks had already risen, it was obvious that the projects were prompting other community greening initiatives. In some cases, ParkWorks' refurbished sites motivated expanded summer garden programs. In others, the sites evolved further, into new performance venues.

Today, as each new state-of-the-art playground is completed, Cleveland's attractiveness as a place to live, work, and raise a family grows. Public school properties, long regarded by many as less than desirable neighbors, are again functioning as centers of attraction.

And the project continues. After achieving substantial early progress, ParkWorks trustees adopted a more ambitious goal than they had originally envisioned. Initially hoping to construct three to five playgrounds each year, the trustees decided instead to try to complete the entire School Grounds as Community Parks initiative within five years. It is a massive undertaking, to be sure, but one well worth the effort and investment. ParkWorks' bold plan promises to make the recreational facilities afforded children in every Cleveland neighborhood the envy of major American cities.

EASTMAN READING GARDEN

A Bit of Heaven

DOWNTOWN CLEVELAND

For an hour or so past its 9 A.M. opening time, you may be delighted to discover that you have the Eastman Reading Garden to yourself. On unseasonably cold mornings at the beginning of May or toward the end of October, this tiny and rare oasis of green in down-

New and improved. The most beloved oasis in downtown Cleveland has recently enjoyed a $1.85 million facelift.

The joy of reading. Artwork specifically commissioned for Eastman Garden is meant to be parsed as well as viewed.

town Cleveland—nestled between the main building and the new Louis Stokes Wing of the Cleveland Public Library—does not begin to fill up until lunchtime. Even on days when the sun's rays are weak, the dedicated brown baggers and passionate readers who work nearby can not be deterred from snatching a few minutes of relaxation or reflection here over their lunch hour. As one regular has stated, office workers flock to Eastman "during a busy and confused day, [to] just sit down and try to collect [their] thoughts and silently be thankful for this small bit of heaven."

However, on mornings when there's a bite to the air, you can while away several hours in Eastman without encountering more than a squadron of crumb-seeking sparrows—that is, if you don't count a wayward bumblebee, lured into the open-air garden by the fall-blooming white rose of sharon that dots its shrub- and tree-filled beds and planters. The naturalistic landscaping (the result of a $1.85 million redesign of the garden completed by the library in 1998 as part of a $100 million restoration and expansion of its downtown campus) helps to break the 100-by-200-foot space into a half-dozen smaller sitting areas and provides welcome shade in the summer. In the chill of late fall it is best not to remain seated for too long; besides, there is plenty to explore.

Eastman is a *reading* garden in more ways than one. Works of public art commissioned specifically for the site are intended to be parsed as well as viewed. Although these artworks are varied in mood and media, all make allusions to the act—and joy—of reading. Created collaboratively by three nationally recognized artists, the works are adorned with letters, syllables, words, and phrases that encourage engagement, inviting you to tease out meaning or compose your own prose poems.

Try, for example, solving the gigantic crossword puzzles that constitute the doors to the massive bronze gates at the ends of the garden, standing open to the street. This is an impossible task, even without the interference of the mischievous bronze figures caught in the act of stealing and rearranging letters on the doors. (Popping up throughout the garden, these playful munchkins are the signature sculpture of New York artist Tom Otterness, creator of the gates.) Or go on a scavenger hunt for whimsical typographic renderings of the wordplay of Virginia poet and Ohio native Tan Lin. You'll find these *Alice in Wonderland*–style evocations cutting a path across the garden's rose and gray granite pavers, playing ring-around-the-rosy on a stone table, and tumbling down the steps of a sunken "room" at the center of the Eastman Reading Garden.

Draw closer and you'll notice that two of the room's walls are formed by an L-shaped fountain of polished charcoal granite. Until the squeal of bus tires frightens them into flight, three pigeons take turns drinking from a shallow-lipped basin of water that spills in slick sheets over the inner edge of the L. The sides of the fountain facing the interior of the room are embossed with yet more lines of Lin's poetry, and his visual puns, carved into the pavers, tickle your feet. Even the title of the fountain, *Reading a Garden,* is written out, in upside-down and reversed steel letters that stand upright on the rear lip of the fountain. The phrase becomes comprehensible only when seen in reflection in the water.

The serene yet undisputed focal point of the garden, this functional sculpture was created by Maya Lin, the Ohio-born artist internationally admired for her design of the Vietnam

Reflections. The centerpiece of the redesigned space is Maya Lin's *Reading a Garden,* a polished granite fountain, with three-dimensional wordplay and softly cascading waters that soothe weary minds.

Veterans Memorial in Washington, D.C. *Reading a Garden,* Lin's first collaboration with her poet-brother, Tan, evokes far different emotions than those inspired by her best-known work. If you perch opposite the fountain on one of the waist-high walls that enclose the room and shut your eyes, you can imagine you are seated on the banks of a mountain brook.

A sharp crunch interrupts a pleasant reverie. A young woman, hair pulled tightly back from a Renaissance face, walks through the garden on her way from Superior to Rockwell, absorbed in a book. She has stepped off the pavers and is strolling through a landscaping bed covered in gravel. Each step produces the satisfying sound of a spoon digging into cereal, but the woman takes no notice of the audible imagery she is creating. Ophelia at her matins?

Toward noon people passing through the garden become more numerous. Intent on reaching another destination, they pull their coat lapels tightly to their chests to block the nipping wind. By 12:30 P.M. fifteen hardy souls have staked out sunny spots in the garden. Most have come by themselves to eat and to read, although a few close their eyes and nap. Then a bespectacled businessman in a navy blue suit and polka-dot tie plops into a black wire chair next to the Maya Lin fountain and opens his briefcase. Out come a sandwich, a bag of chips, and a soda, which are placed one by one on the lip of the fountain. With table secured, Mr. Hornrims lunches while perusing the sports section of the *Plain Dealer.* Public

A Bit of Heaven

Mischief makers. Whether stealing letters from the garden's signature gates or caught in the act of eavesdropping, Tom Otterness's bronze figurines add a delightful touch of whimsy.

art as patio furniture? The incongruous scene testifies to the ease with which these amiable artworks blend into their surroundings and contribute to the relaxed, welcoming atmosphere of this singular place.

Eastman Reading Garden may never have been as highly designed as it is today, but it has always been a popular retreat. Throughout its sixty-four-year lifespan the garden has served to remind us that even the smallest open space can be put to significant public use. Satisfying the public's appetite for outdoor recreation does not necessarily require vast expanses or strenuous exertion. A spot of green in which to stretch one's legs, catch a breath of fresh air, or enjoy a moment's peace, within walking distance of home or office, is an easily provided urban amenity. All it took to create this pocket park originally was a little gumption. The city of Cleveland acquired the empty lot, planted grass and a few shrubs and trees, and set out some benches. (Could this idea be tested in a few strategic sites to determine its merits as a low-cost, low-tech way of dealing with the pervasive urban problem of abandoned lots?)

The land that became the Eastman Reading Garden was, to be precise, assembled in two stages. The first parcel was purchased from East Ohio Gas Company in 1913 as part of the continuing implementation of Chicago architect Daniel Burnham's 1903 Group Plan for downtown Cleveland, commissioned by Progressive mayor Tom L. Johnson. Burnham had recommended that an open square be created at the corner of Superior and East 6th Street next to an envisioned Beaux Arts building meant to house the municipal library. This new park would be a mirror image of the individual quadrants of Public Square to the west of the library, just as a proposed new federal courthouse would echo the design of the library, its next-door neighbor to the east. The American Progressive movement that inspired Eastman Park embraced a classical conception of beauty.

Twelve years passed before the Main Library building was finally constructed—its unveiling marking another triumph for the Cleveland architectural firm of Walker & Weeks (designers of the Federal Reserve Bank one block to the east)—and, by then, the Plain Dealer Publishing Company occupied most of the remaining land intended for Burnham's open square. Still seeking to realize Tom Johnson's vision of Cleveland as a "city on a hill," municipal administrators purchased a narrow strip of land adjoining the 1913 parcel to the east of the new Main Library from the newspaper company. The purchase agreement stipulated that the property be forever preserved in its undeveloped state in exchange for the company's promise not to expand its physical plant beyond the height of the adjacent Group Plan buildings.

After painstakingly assembling the parkland, the city of Cleveland did nothing immediately to improve it. The two empty parcels, acquired for a total purchase price of $540,000, served for another dozen years primarily as a convenient but unkempt shortcut between Superior and Rockwell. Then, with the Depression lifting in 1937, a concrete walkway and simple seating were installed.

Modest though they were, these new amenities caught the eye of Linda Anne Eastman, the director of the Cleveland Public Library and one of the most visionary public servants ever to grace the local scene. Then seventy years old and nearing the end of her two-decade tenure as the only female head of a major U.S. metropolitan library, Miss Eastman made a decision that was to enhance the recreational assets of Greater Clevelanders for generations to come. She determined to turn the humble little park into an outdoor reading room similar to the one in Bryant Park that served the patrons of the New York Public Library.

This was only her most visible contribution. In 1892, when Miss Eastman began her career as an assistant at the first branch of the Cleveland Public Library (on Pearl Street, now West 25th), librarians wore starched white aprons; their demeanor was stiffer still. When not

A Bit of Heaven

busy checking books in and out of the locked glass cases in which they were kept, librarians occupied themselves with embroidery and crocheting. After rising through the ranks, she was appointed library director in 1918, upon the untimely death of her predecessor, William Howard Brett. Although she had not sought her position of leadership, Miss Eastman moved to professionalize the organization, expanding Brett's open-shelf policy; instituting specialized services for children, the blind, and the hospitalized; supervising the construction of the Main Library building; and helping to plan the curriculum of the library school at Western Reserve University. "Books are as nourishing as food" was the philosophy that guided her creation of Cleveland's modern library system, which grew from 18 employees and 58,000 books to 1,100 employees and more than two million volumes during her forty-six years of service.

Although the library's resources had been badly strained by the Great Depression, Miss Eastman managed to equip the new outdoor reading room with a table, two chairs (for the comfort of the librarians who were on duty from noon to two), a bookcase, and a magazine rack, all of which were painted green and covered by a brightly colored beach umbrella. Open for business in the summer of 1937, the outdoor reading room had only donated magazines and worn-out books, but they were made available to anyone who asked, regardless of whether the borrower possessed a library card. That September, Cleveland City Council voted to name the little park in honor of the distinguished head of the Cleveland Public Library, whose staff continued to fine-tune service by soliciting local merchants for additional beach umbrellas to shade the patrons and by creating a reserved seating section for the fairer sex. "Most women prefer not to sit on the same bench with men or even on a bench next to them," explained an internal library memo. "The same thing is true of children."

By the 1940s and '50s, behavior in Eastman Park had truly sunk to levels most persons found objectionable. Vagrants, drunks, and lovers were taking over the premises after dark and leaving behind a blanket of rubbish that discouraged normal use during the daylight hours. In 1959 the library sought to lease Eastman Park from the city for the nominal payment of one dollar a year, with the intention of refurbishing the space and fencing it off. Entrance to the proposed new Eastman Reading Garden would be gained only through the old Plain Dealer building, which the library had purchased in 1957 for use as a business and science annex. The city objected to the proposed restrictions, and a compromise was struck that preserved public access to the garden. The Friends of the Library, a group of the city's social and civic elite who were undertaking the garden's renovation as a do-it-yourself project, agreed to install gates in the iron fencing they proposed to erect at the open ends of the garden.

Under the care of the Friends, the Eastman Reading Garden blossomed into the most beautiful and beloved green space in downtown Cleveland. With financial support from three blue-chip family funds (the Louis D. Beaumont Foundation, the Leonard C. Hanna, Jr., Fund, and the Elizabeth Ring Mather and William Gwinn Mather Fund) and The Cleveland Foundation, the garden was professionally landscaped with pink flowering crabapple, shade-providing gum trees, and lush beds of English ivy. For the more prominent south entrance, Friends chairperson Marjorie (Mrs. Robert H.) Jamison secured a decorative wrought-iron gate by master European craftsmen from a home for unwed mothers on Euclid Avenue that had once been the Francis Drury estate. A splashing wall fountain, two large jardinieres that had once belonged to Leonard C. Hanna, and a bronze armillary sundial on a green marble pedestal were donated. These adornments were supplemented by pots of geraniums in the summer and chrysanthemums in the fall, lovingly supplied by Mrs. Jamison's fellow members of the Shaker Lakes Garden Club.

To complete the transformation, the Friends saw to it that a selection of recorded classical music was played in the garden during the noon hour. One day, when a semiclassical number was slipped into the program, a regular garden patron dashed off a letter of protest to the library administration. "Let those who prefer the wishy-washy shilly-shallying of Montovani and his ilk repair to the restaurants where they will be fed Muzak with their meals; let those who prefer the raucous sounds of modern music linger in the juke-box joints or enjoy themselves while waiting for the Rapid cars in the Terminal," the distraught West Sider wrote in June 1960, a month after the Eastman Reading Garden opened, "but please, let us, the minority, have this one haven of refuge in the midst of noise and dissension."

The extent to which the citizens of Greater Cleveland were devoted to this "haven of refuge" became overwhelmingly apparent in 1989, when the library unveiled plans for what was to become its new Louis Stokes Wing. To gain space for improved services and storage, architects Hardy Holzman Pfeiffer Associates of New York and URS Consultants of Cleveland recommended that a new tower be built over the garden's airspace, a move that would

A Bit of Heaven

The lunch bunch. Eastman regulars range from business executives to construction workers.

have turned Eastman into a climate-controlled atrium. Historic preservationists and representatives of the thousand or so downtown workers estimated to congregate there on a typical summer's day organized a "Save Eastman Garden" campaign. The group, operating informally out of The Trust for Public Land's Cleveland office, circulated petitions, sent out mailings protesting the plan, proselytized the media, and lobbied the library's trustees. Cleveland's mayor at the time, George V. Voinovich, joined the preservationists' cause, reminding the library of the city's promise never to allow development of the property.

Reevaluating its priorities, the library modified its expansion plans to ensure that Eastman Reading Garden would not only be preserved, but that it would get a complete makeover. (The appearance of the garden had last been freshened in the early 1980s.) Although some might have been content with a redesign that merely did no harm, the library made excellence its objective. In this time of meritocracy, expert hands guided the renovation. The library retained the well-regarded Olin Partnership of Philadelphia to reconceive the garden's landscaping and asked the Committee for Public Art (now Cleveland Public Art), a not-for-profit organization dedicated to facilitating the creation of site-specific art for public spaces, to undertake a national search for artists capable of contributing a distinctive personal stamp. This time the voters of Cleveland, who in 1991 had overwhelmingly approved a bond issue to pay for the library expansion, provided the wherewithal.

Eastman Reading Garden

Love letters. Messages inscribed in commemorative pavers convey what this space no bigger than a basketball court means to a large cross-section of Greater Cleve-landers.

The library's invitation to the public to provide further support for the redesign through the purchase of commemorative paving stones added yet another dimension to the multi-layered experience of *reading a garden* achieved by the professionals. When you wander through Eastman on a brisk October day, examining the messages carved in the pavers, you feel almost as if you're searching for ancestral headstones in some windswept country cemetery. Yet it's not a melancholy enterprise. On the contrary, you come away uplifted by the sense of what this space no bigger than a basketball court means to a large cross-section of Greater Clevelanders.

Some pavers identify the garden's fans: "ITT Hartford Group Ins./Property Casualty Ins." or "The Cleveland Ursulines" or "Phillip C. Holmes/The World's Best Daddy." Another proclaims the garden to be "Our Favorite Place/Kenly and Susan Murray." The Save Eastman Garden paver quotes American philosopher Bronson Alcott (the father of novelist Louisa May Alcott), who believed "Who loves a garden still his eden keeps." Another sentiment captures the spirit of time passed in Eastman Reading Garden: "May Peace and Tolerance," pray Phil, Jane, Sam, and Abby, "Grow Like A Garden."

CUYAHOGA VALLEY
NATIONAL PARK

Preserving the Panorama of the Past Twelve Thousand Years

BOSTON TOWNSHIP

Two miles south of Peninsula, Ohio, on Riverview Road in Boston Township, lies the cross-roads settlement of Everett. Most drivers speed past this collection of unremarkable buildings —frame homes, a few garages, an abandoned gas station—without recognizing that they are in the presence of something unique.

Nor are they likely to realize that Everett is a valued part of the Cuyahoga Valley National Park, a unit of the National Park Service (NPS) that was established to conserve thirty-three thousand acres of flood plain, forested slope, and upland plateau flanking a scenic two-mile stretch of the Cuyahoga River from Akron to Independence. Each year more than three million visitors are attracted to this "big green garden" (as park superintendent John Debo describes it), an attendance figure that places the Cuyahoga Valley National Park (CVNP) in the ranks of the top twenty most popular national parks in the country.

The park's creation in 1974 guaranteed the preservation of the valley's diverse *cultural* landscapes, as well. As users of the Towpath Trail that runs the length of the CVNP from north to south are well aware, the park contains an integral part of a nationally important example of nineteenth-century transportation infrastructure: a partially watered section of the Ohio & Erie Canal encompassing sixteen locks. Far fewer people are aware that some

Outdoor museum. Hundreds of historic sites, structures, and artifacts within the CVNP boundaries, such as the millstone pictured here, tell the story of human habitation of the Cuyahoga River Valley. Had it not been for a coalition of preservationists who pushed for the park's creation, these irreplaceable resources might have fallen victim to urban development.

223 known archeological sites, 250 historic buildings, 26 canal structures, and 4 bridges also lie within the CVNP boundaries. These irreplaceable resources include the site where, in the late eighteenth century, Moravian missionaries established the first known Euro-American settlement along the Cuyahoga River and an early-twentieth-century company town called Jaite, built to house employees of a valley paper mill. Taken as a whole, these assets tell the story of human habitation of the Cuyahoga River Valley from the time of its creation by retreating glaciers twelve thousand years ago through the Industrial Age.

Not surprisingly, some of the especially rich holdings from the canal era have been restored. At Lock 38, near the intersection of Canal and Hillside Roads in Independence, visitors can poke around an 1820s public house and general store that has been restored for use as an information center for the park and the canal. Legend has it that this establishment

Everett, Ohio. The seemingly unremarkable collection of buildings that sprang up at the intersection of Everett and Riverview Roads in Boston Township is a nationally important example of a fading piece of Americana: the hamlet.

had a colorful reputation among canal travelers as "Hell's Half Acre." At a refurbished warehouse in Boston, Ohio—once a major center of canal boat–building activity, now a sleepy village—visitors can learn how these sturdy craft were constructed. Near a turning basin on Canal Road they can marvel at the elegance and ingenuity of Stephen Frazee's Federal farmhouse, built by hand in 1826 from 100,000 locally pressed bricks. Frazee may well have paid for this handsome dwelling with the $130 he received in compensation for water damage to his crops incurred during construction of the canal.

Efforts by the CVNP to illuminate bygone days in the valley should be considered a work in progress, however. With renovation of historic buildings and locales dependent on the vagaries of federal funding, many potential attractions are not yet open to the public. The prehistoric archeological sites may never be. At least, with the CVNP as their protector, the valley's "hidden" treasures are no longer in danger of falling victim to urban sprawl or neglect.

Perhaps nowhere in the park is the historic cultural landscape more textured than around the seemingly nondescript intersection of Everett and Riverview Roads. The crossroads area is part of four different districts that have merited inclusion on the National Register of Historic Places. Each district illuminates a distinct era of valley land use. To stroll around Everett is to take a self-guided tour of not one, but several panoramas of our vanished agrarian past.

"Johnnycake Lock." Everett is the location of Lock 27 of the Ohio & Erie Canal. The origin of its nickname, a reference to a type of cornbread, is a puzzle.

Visitors turning west onto Everett Road from Riverview will eventually traverse a low, slightly sloping terrace of land that drops off into a field across the road from the Everett Church of Christ. This terrace, called Everett Knoll, is listed on the National Register. Archeologists believe it to be the remains of a prehistoric ceremonial mound that was either constructed or sculpted from a natural land form around A.D. 300. The mound builders could have practiced subsistence farming on the muddy banks of Furnace Run Creek (a tributary of the Cuyahoga River) to the south, although no cultivated plant remains have been found to date. Evidence that has been uncovered—stone projectile points and flakes, charred animal bones, and nut hulls—suggests that Everett was once home to two Hopewellian habitation sites.

If visitors going south on Riverview look to the left when passing the intersection of Everett Road, through a gap between two houses they might see the remnants of the Ohio & Erie Canal (a section of which between Rockside Road and Route 82 is a National Register Historic District). Everett is the location of Lock 27, also known as "Johnnycake Lock." The origin of the name is clouded, but it may refer to the cornbread diet of canal boat passengers left stranded after Furnace Run flooded in 1828, shutting down navigation between Cleveland and Akron. That was as far as the canal stretched by that date; it would be 1832 before the canal builders reached the Ohio River.

When completed, the canal opened up important new markets to farmers, as well as to

Preserving the Panorama

emerging businesses and industry, throughout Ohio, creating a trade boom that transformed a frontier state into the third wealthiest member of the Union. Settlers of the Western Reserve who once raised corn and pigs for their own consumption rushed to plant wheat and to breed cattle, as surpluses of these commodities could be now be shipped to market and turned into cash. South of Everett, the Western Reserve Historical Society operates the canal-era Hale Farm and Village. Like the Frazee House, Jonathan Hale's Federal farmhouse was built in 1826 of local bricks. The signature building of this living museum, it too reflects the rising fortunes of valley farmers.

Nevertheless, the richest man along Furnace Run may have been an entrepreneur named Alanson Swan, a member of the booming service economy that sprang up canalside to facilitate every aspect of the processing and transport of goods. At Johnnycake Lock in what was then known as Unionville Swan operated a grocery store, warehouse, and livery stable for the care and exchange of the mules that towed the canal boats by ropes from the towpath next to the water. These enterprises are gone, but until its recent demolition Swan's home (built in 1818 by Henry Iddings, the first pioneer to settle in the vicinity of Everett) still stood on Riverview Road. Excavations around the partially collapsed building, once the oldest structure in Everett, uncovered evidence of whiteware dishes—a sign of prosperity.

The coming of the railroads may have ended the dominance of the canal, but they put Unionville on the map. In 1880, business interests seeking to tap coalfields in central Ohio built the Valley Railway from Cleveland to Canton and on into Tuscarawas County. The railroad line established a depot in Uniontown, renaming the stop Everett after Sylvester Everett, the secretary-treasurer of the company. Today cars entering or leaving Everett on Riverview Road bump across the tracks of the Valley Railway line, a National Register Historic District that now serves as an excursion route for the Cuyahoga Valley Scenic Railroad.

The advent of a general post office in Everett, also in 1880, assured that the station stop would in time grow into a hamlet. As a piece of Americana that has now gone the way of the drugstore soda fountain and the five-cent cigar, Everett has won its own listing as a National Register Historic District.

Defined by their lack of internal streets and a tiny radius (typically, no more than a quarter of a mile), hamlets were at one time the smallest and most ubiquitous type of settlement in rural America, except for farmsteads, which hamlets sprang up to serve. Within a

End of the line.
The coming of railroads ended the dominance of the canal. Today the Cuyahoga Valley Scenic Railroad offers excursions on the old Valley Railway line built between Cleveland and Canton.

decade of the Valley Railway's construction, Everett was almost too bustling to be considered one of this breed. By 1888 it boasted a population of two hundred residents and such service-oriented businesses as a general store with a restaurant and poolroom, a hotel, a livery stable and feed store, and a Western Union Telegraph office—all scattered randomly about as if thrown from a die cup. A one-room schoolhouse had been part of the community since the 1840s. The citizens of Everett included an auctioneer, a blacksmith, a music teacher, a saloon keeper, a carpenter, and one A. A. Richardson, identified in a county directory as "postmaster, bridge builder and pile driver."

Farmers whose fields surrounded Everett were considered members of the community. One such family was headed by Norman and Martha Hunt. In 1867 the Hunts purchased land to the east of the canal on both sides of Furnace Run. Here the Hunts and some of their thirteen children raised row crops and grain until the turn of the century. The Hunts' modest 1880 farmhouse on Bolanz Road serves as a CVNP visitor and information center. On display are excerpts from the oral history of a woman born on the old Hunt homestead in the 1920s. She describes the lack of running water, the kerosene lamps, and the coal heating stoves that typified domestic life on valley farms in the years immediately preceding the Depression. Electricity came to Everett only in 1931.

The Reverend John Fisk of the Church in the Valley in Everett. By the late 1880s Everett boasted a population of two hundred residents whose material needs were met by a general store with a restaurant and poolroom, a livery stable, and feed store. Today the church is Everett's only active enterprise.

The year before, Sager's Gas Station and Confectionery opened on the southwest corner of Everett Road and Riverview—another sign of progress. However, the arrival of the automobile and the rise of paved roads freed rural Americans from their dependence on businesses located at a nearby crossroads. By the mid-1970s, when CVNP managers began purchasing every parcel of land available within the park's boundaries, Everett's population had dwindled to a few dozen. In the mid-1980s the park purchased most of the property around the crossroads from the remaining residents, with an eye to turning the hamlet into the home of an artists-in-residence program. When that idea failed to gel, critics lambasted the CVNP's aggressive land acquisition program for creating a ghost town. It was not the first time that the park managers had come under fire for pressuring valley residents and landowners to sell property for which the CVNP seemed to have no clear use.

By contrast, the present administration has encouraged people to live on and even gently work the land, a potentially revolutionary approach to parklands management that has helped to end controversy and soothe bad feelings. And the passage of time has made the park's past practice of land banking look farsighted, especially in the case of Everett.

In the nineteenth century there were seven hamlets within or near the boundaries of the present-day CVNP. Today only two remain: Everett, and Hammond's Corners at Route 21 and Ira Road in Bath Township. The other five hamlets have disappeared under concrete and asphalt, and modern construction detracts from the historic appearance of Hammond's

Jonathan Hale's Federal farmhouse. Built in 1826 of locally made bricks, the signature building of Hale Farm and Village testifies to the rising prosperity that accompanied the building of the canal.

Corners. Only Everett, where the buildings retain their original scale and varying setbacks and where modern renovations have been minimal, remains. To wander through the quiet hamlet, across grassy lawns and under spreading trees that shade old-time privies and chicken coops, in a loop that leads back to the silent Sager's filling station is to return to an era when the Valley Railway made a daily stop to pick up farmers' milk bound for city markets and to drop off the mail . . . when people walked to the general store if they wanted to make a phone call . . . when the basement of the church echoed with the laughter of penny suppers and quilting parties. The picture of life in and around Everett would have been less vivid had not the park stepped forward to acquire the hamlet.

While many of the old buildings in Everett have now been renovated for park administrative use, efforts to preserve the historic landscapes of the valley have not focused entirely on bricks and mortar. After becoming the park's third superintendent in 1988, John P. Debo, Jr., recognized that small-scale farming in the valley was itself becoming a rare cultural tradition. Debo began looking for ways to reseed this once-dominant valley enterprise, but it was not until he went on sabbatical in England that he found the inspiration he sought.

In Britain Debo was struck by the fact that approximately 90 percent of the land in the national park system is privately owned and used for agricultural purposes. Upon his return to this country, Debo set about applying the insight that parks could offer the enjoyment

Preserving the Panorama

A demonstration of nineteenth-century plowing techniques at Hale Farm. Efforts to preserve the cultural landscapes of the Valley have not focused exclusively on bricks and mortar.

of working farms among their recreational opportunities. In 1998 the CVNP encouraged creation of a not-for-profit organization called the Cuyahoga Countryside Conservancy to provide the conceptual and technical assistance needed to revitalize old farms owned by the park. The conservancy would also assist with the leasing of this fallow but still viable farmland to persons interested in practicing sustainable agriculture.

Under the direction of Darwin Kelsey, a former agricultural historian and curator who was the first administrator of Lake Farmpark (a unit of the Lake Metroparks system in Kirtland, Ohio), the conservancy identified thirty valley farmsteads comprising approximately 1,500 acres that it hopes over time to return to productive use. In the year 2000, Kelsey began to interview and recruit individuals and families who had applied to intensively care for small plots of park land on which they propose to raise high-quality fruits, vegetables, and livestock (without, needless to say, heavy reliance on pesticides). The idea is that visitors to the park will be able to observe up close the activities of an endangered species—the family farm —while serving as the primary market for the farms' products. This promises to be a win-win relationship. If so, the conservancy's prototype program could redefine policy and practices throughout the national park system, where many park managers are struggling to preserve historic farming landscapes using park maintenance crews.

Practicing sustainable agriculture. Cuyahoga Valley National Park actively encourages "smart" farming within its boundaries. Here, Kathleen Varga, proprietor of the Crooked River Herb Farm in Boston Township, tends her lemon verbena.

THE PERPETUATION OF farming as a significant part of the history of Cuyahoga River Valley was probably not one of the original goals of Akron Metropolitan Park Board, a three-member body established in 1921, in emulation of the Cleveland Metroparks model. Nevertheless, the idea of preserving the picturesque, rural character of the Cuyahoga River Valley emerged from the Akron park board's early activities.

As one of its first official acts, the Akron park board commissioned the landscape architectural firm founded by Frederick Law Olmsted to survey the scenic assets of Summit County and to make recommendations about which locations had the greatest potential to become recreational resources. The choice of Olmsted Brothers had been influenced by park board member and rubber industry leader Frank A. Seiberling, who became acquainted with the firm's work when he retained a former partner of Olmsted's to design the grounds of his Akron estate, Stan Hywet.

Olmsted Brothers's 1925 report declared Summit County's premier natural feature to be the Cuyahoga River Valley. The report recommended (among other things) that the Akron park board acquire land to build one or more pleasure drives leading from the city through the valley and attempt to preserve the remainder of the landscape as far north as Furnace Run, using scenic easements to restrict its use. Lack of funds and authority prevented the park board from realizing this ambitious vision, although both the Akron parks system (today's

A win-win situation. Park visitors can observe up close the activities of an endangered species—the family farm—while serving as the primary market for the farm's products.

Metro Parks, Serving Summit County) and Cleveland Metroparks ultimately established several reservations each in the valley.

The next step forward came in the late 1960s, when the concept of conserving the valley in its entirety gained a powerful proponent in Akron lawyer John F. Seiberling. As a boy Seiberling had enjoying hiking and horseback riding in the valley, which his grandfather F. A. Seiberling's estate overlooked. In fact, the Seiberling family fortunes were inextricably linked to the valley. Its farmers had helped fuel the growth of the Seiberling Company, maker of Empire mowers and reapers, into one of the largest harvesting-machine manufacturers in the world by the century's turn. Seiberling had both sentimental and—in his capacity as president of the regional planning commission for Summit, Portage, and Medina Counties —civic reasons for fighting various developments in the valley. Finding himself on the losing side of those battles, Seiberling went to Columbus to persuade Governor James A. Rhodes to do something about the situation. Rhodes asked the Ohio Department of Natural Resources (ODNR) to conduct a study.

In 1968 ODNR reported back that it had reached the "indisputable conclusion" that at least ten thousand acres in the Cuyahoga River Valley must be conserved as public open space and that the rural character of another thirteen thousand acres must be protected by scenic easements. The report recommended that the Akron and Cleveland park districts work together to preserve the land, but by now it had become clear to Seiberling and others that only the federal government had the resources to intervene successfully. Former Cleveland congressman Charles Vanik subsequently persuaded Stewart Udall, then U.S. secretary of the interior, to tour the valley in 1967. Udall left impressed with the beauty of the landscape, but puzzled as to where the mixed-used acreage would fit into the NPS classification system.

So matters stood until Akron sent John Seiberling to Congress in 1970. As almost his first act in office, Seiberling drafted a bill authorizing the establishment of a national park in the Cuyahoga River Valley. The coalition of concerned citizens and officials who supported such a proposal had reached critical mass, making its voice hard to ignore. Nonetheless, during Seiberling's first term in office, his colleagues in Congress remained unmoved by the vision and arguments of the park's proponents. Persisting with his lobbying efforts during his second term, Seiberling finally rounded up sufficient votes in favor of establishing a park in the valley under a newly created NPS classification: "urban national recreation area." At the time there were only two such parks in America. The Cuyahoga Valley National Recreation Area was reclassified as a national park in October 2000.

The Debo administration has recognized and taken full advantage of this opportunity to define a new kind of national park, one that celebrates and champions land that is neither totally developed nor totally wild. Darwin Kelsey notes that the British call this in-between space the "middle landscape." Perhaps because we have no name for it, America is allowing its middle landscape—forests and wetlands, farms and hamlets, villages and small towns, and all the lives and activities that they shelter—to be chewed up by new development. Thanks to the Cuyahoga Valley National Park and the civic visionaries who pushed for the park's creation, Greater Clevelanders can revel in a dynamic middle landscape of national significance.

MENTOR LAGOONS NATURE PRESERVE AND MARINA

A Miraculous Save

LAKE COUNTY

The twenty-five or so people gathered in the parking lot of the Mentor Lagoons Nature Preserve and Marina on a Saturday morning in October were mostly middle-aged men and women, but ready for adventure nevertheless. They had risen early to go on a nature walk,

Terra incognita. Mentor Lagoons Preserve has opened for public enjoyment a formerly off-limits remnant of the upland forests that once covered Ohio.

Walking encyclopedia. Cleveland Museum of Natural History botanist Jim Bissell identifies one of the three hundred species of plants that have already been inventoried in the preserve.

one of the featured activities of Coastweeks, an annual celebration of Lake Erie in which the lakeshore city of Mentor, Ohio, was participating. This was to be no ordinary walk in the park, however. The guide was perhaps the leading expert on native Ohio plants—Jim Bissell, chief curator of botany at the Cleveland Museum of Natural History and a champion and protector of the adjacent Mentor Marsh. Bissell's destination: terra incognita.

The nature walk would pass through three lake plain habitats that until recently had been private property off limits to the public. The explorers would set off in deep, second-growth woodlands, a thriving remnant of upland forests of oak, maple, beech, and chestnut that had covered Ohio before the first white settlers arrived. Red and black oaks between three and four feet in diameter and hundred-year-old cucumber magnolias could be viewed there. The group would then wend its way down into the dunes that fringed a 1.5-mile-long stretch of wild beach. In these two distinct habitats the explorers would be on the lookout for rare coastal plants. The possibility of spotting species that are threatened or endangered in Ohio was good. With only 40 of the state's 262 miles of Lake Erie shoreline in public hands and only 6.5 miles of it publicly accessible, Mentor Lagoons Nature Preserve and Marina contains the largest untouched beach remaining between Cleveland and the Pennsylvania state line.

The beach was about a mile away from the marina parking lot. It was only a twenty-

A Miraculous Save

minute walk down the Lakefront Trail, a former road that the city of Mentor had transformed into a hiking and biking path after it assembled the 450-acre property in 1997 and 1998. Yet nearly two hours would elapse before the Bissell expedition emerged from the forest onto an open ridge and caught sight of a blue wedge of lake topped by a perfectly clear sky in which a bevy of white sails danced.

Although the woodlands terrain was level—evidence that today's uplands had been yesterday's lake bed—the walk proceeded slowly. Even though he knew that bigger surprises lay ahead on the beach—having surveyed the entire Mentor Marsh ecosystem in an effort to document and protect its flora—Bissell could not restrain himself from stopping every minute or two to comment on a tree, shrub, or perennial that he found interesting growing alongside the path. He had his choice of more than three hundred species of plants on which to focus, according to a botanical inventory of the preserve the city of Mentor had conducted the previous year with the help of the volunteer Lagoons Nature Corps.

An elfin man with a sharp nose, blue eyes, and curly blond hair crammed underneath a brown baseball cap emblazoned with the Natural History Museum logo, Jim Bissell was a walking encyclopedia of plant lore. "That's white snakeroot," he said, pointing to a green leafy stalk that to the untrained eye looked like a weed. "It's a common woodland plant that cows like to eat. It causes milk sickness. Lincoln's mother died from that." Further down the path he discovered a white ash, "a member of the olive family," Bissell observed. "It's the wood they use in baseball bats." By the time the group began its descent down the open ridge, with its own distinct colony of plants, and into the dunes, Bissell was covered in burrs. Some two dozen times he had crawled into the understory along the path to identify and describe specimens ranging from native impatiens to the silver maple, formerly the dominant tree in the swamp forests that were once a common feature of the lake plain and of which Mentor Marsh is one of the last remaining examples.

Bissell could have had a successful career as an entertainer. Materializing a magnifying loop in the middle of the walk, he demonstrated how to tell a grass from a sedge (the former has a round stem, the latter's base is triangular). Encountering what he hoped was a native viburnum, he pulled off a leaf and popped it into his mouth. Its palatability confirmed that the bush was indeed indigenous. A bitter taste would have signaled that the viburnum was a Japanese exotic, introduced into the state by nurseries unaware that non-native species

Taking the measure of a trailside plant. The size of the berries will tell Bissell whether a specimen is Tuckman's panic grass.

from Europe or Asia, being more aggressive than their Ohio counterparts, turn into invasive killers. Bissell's ongoing field surveys of virtually every important natural habitat in northern Ohio make him a major contributor to the upkeep of the state of Ohio's listing of endangered and threatened plants. He exhorted the assemblage to "love your natives."

As the group walked through the dunes toward the driftwood-covered beach, Bissell stopped to admire the beach grass. Without its sand-trapping properties there would be fewer and smaller dunes along the eastern seaboard. The group then focused its attention on another switch grass, a former prairie dweller. "Now we're in a new world," Bissell proclaimed as the group stepped out onto flatter ground between the sandy beach and the dunes. The "foredunes," as Bissell termed the area, bristled with vines, grasses, berry bushes, and even fungi.

The group barely had time to note the seaside spurge ("related to the poinsettia") or the horse-tail ("also known as scouring rushes") before an excited Bissell was bending over another specimen. "This is an endangered grass in Ohio—coastal little bluestem; that's purple sand grass—it's potentially threatened," he said, rapid-fire. "The sea rocket over there is potentially threatened, too. You're surrounded by rare plants."

"What are we going to do about it?" someone asked, referring to the loss of lakeshore habitat.

A Miraculous Save

Plant watching. The new preserve protects the largest untouched beach between Cleveland and the Pennsylvania state line, where threatened and endangered species such as purple sandgrass, sea rocket, and beach pea can be spotted.

"We're going to enjoy them," Bissell responded, moving closer to a massive stand of low-lying leafy vines. "Boy, is it a good year for beach pea," he noted. "We've walked by more of it this morning than I've seen anywhere else in years. Oh, here, we've got one in flower. Isn't that gorgeous? I've never been close enough before to sniff it."

"Are they edible?" someone inquired about the flowers of the beach pea, which are actually light- to dark-purple pods.

"Yeah, but you shouldn't eat them," Bissell warned. "They're threatened in Ohio. We're losing so many specimens before we even know they're here."

Preservation of natural habitats—for public enjoyment and scientific study—is, of course, one of many important functions a modern park can serve. The Mentor Lagoons Nature Preserve was created to maintain public access and inhibit development. Private developers have longed to transform the land into a resort property since the mid-1920s, when a syndicate of Cleveland businessmen led by S. Livingston Mather purchased from the Baltimore & Ohio Railroad 750 lakefront acres on which to build a yacht and beach club surrounded by private housing. (Earlier the site had been eyed for industrial use.) Before the Depression put an end to the businessmen's dream of replicating Florida's Lido Venice Club in Lake County, the syndicate dredged the far western edge of the marsh at its nexus with Lake Erie and constructed concrete basins to create boat lagoons.

Mentor Marsh. The seven-hundred-acre habitat is the largest wetlands remaining on Lake Erie.

In the 1950s the next owner proposed to turn the property into a thousand-home development complete with a nine-hole golf course and a marina big enough to accommodate five thousand pleasure craft. Litigation forestalled the grandiose scheme for more than a decade. When the Ohio Supreme Court ruled in 1966 that the lagoons were a public asset (even though many of the lots abutting the waterway had been purchased by private citizens), it was the first step toward preservation of the largely intact B & O parcel. This was the last acreage needed to create a 1,300-acre band of green near the lakeshore in fast-growing Lake County.

Today this "Lake Erie Corridor" encompasses a variety of open spaces, the best known of which is Headlands Beach State Park, at the northern terminus of State Route 44. Now a regional recreational asset with the longest public swimming beach in Ohio, the state park attracts 800,000 swimmers, sunbathers, and picnickers annually.

To the east and southwest of Headlands Beach are two other nature preserves: Headlands Dunes State Nature Preserve, another fine beach habitat that is home (like the Lagoons Preserve) to plant species typically found only along the Atlantic Coast, and Mentor Marsh State Nature Preserve, an extremely significant wetlands. These two public lands are related through their geology and hydrology (although the "plumbing" of the headlands, through which run the Grand River and such tributaries as Blackbrook Creek, is only partially

A day in the sun.
Headlands Beach
State Park in Mentor
attracts 800,000
swimmers and
picnickers every
year.

understood). Had the acreage that is now the Mentor Lagoons Nature Preserve and Marina fallen victim to long-intended development, the loss would have had adverse consequences for the entire watershed, but especially for the extremely rich and diverse plant communities supported by its multiplicity of habitats.

The conservation effort began in earnest on the headlands in the early 1960s and centered first on Mentor Marsh—with good reason. At nearly seven hundred acres, Mentor Marsh is the largest wetlands remaining near Lake Erie in a state that has lost nearly 85 percent of this natural resource. Long before it became unique, the marsh attracted the attention of naturalists. As early as the 1840s, Cleveland physician Jared Potter Kirtland tramped its banks, making detailed records of the bird life he observed there. Around the turn of the century the Burroughs Nature Club, founded in Willoughby, Ohio, rediscovered the charms of the area on its spring nature hikes. Club member Charles M. Shipman was the first to propose that the marsh be preserved. A chemist inspired by the love of nature, Shipman advocated in the 1930s that the state acquire the marsh, as well as the beach and sand dunes on the headlands, for a public park. A pond at the northeastern end of the marsh bears his name.

The lakefront park became a reality in 1951, but the fate of the marsh was not decided until a decade later. In 1961, as part of a parks master plan for Lake County, officials proposed to dredge the marsh so that it could be used as a recreational waterway. Outraged,

Burroughs Nature Club president Harold J. Zimmerman garnered the support and resources needed to set aside 619 acres of the marsh in 1965 under the management of the Cleveland Museum of Natural History. Six years later, Mentor Marsh was among the first four natural areas to be incorporated into the state's new system of nature preserves. The fascinating story of the complex series of land acquisitions and surface rights negotiations that saved Mentor Marsh from heedless destruction has already been told in an excellent pamphlet available at the preserve's nature center on Corduroy Road near State Route 283. Suffice it to note here that Zimmerman Trail, the longest hiking trail in the preserve, was named in honor of the man who launched this heroic campaign.

In 1966 the conservation movement in Lake County received another boost when the U.S. Department of the Interior declared Mentor Marsh a National Natural Landmark in recognition of its "exceptional value in illustrating the natural history of the United States."

Radiocarbon dating of sediment samples taken recently by University of Akron geologists from fourteen feet down in the muck revealed that the marsh is more than two thousand years old. It is the product of the Grand River, whose change in course thousands of years ago slowly cut a new mouth into Lake Erie some four miles east of the river's former delta. As the old channel filled with plant debris, it became the fertile medium in which an open cattail marsh and then a swamp forest grew. Thirty-six species of deciduous trees still grew in the channel and on its slopes in the mid-1960s. But the swamp forest was by then well on its way to reverting to marsh. Salt tailings accidentally released into Blackbrook Creek in the late 1950s raised the salinity of the water flowing through the marsh to levels that eventually killed the trees.

In such a hostile environment only one plant really thrived: *phragmites australis,* or salt-marsh grass, a flowering plant capable of growing to twelve feet tall in a single year. The phragmites grew so thick and spread so quickly that, over time, most of the marshland became nearly impenetrable. With the exception of Shipman Pond at the northernmost end and Becker Pond at the southeastern end, Mentor Marsh may now appear to some eyes to be a forbidding, dead place.

The operative word is "appear." The marsh is alive with some 125 species of birds, as well as insects, amphibians, and small mammals, including ermine and mink. (Wildlife is best glimpsed—or heard—near the ponds at dawn and dusk, according to marsh naturalist Nancy

Csider.) And preliminary satellite mapping by The University of Akron geologists shows that the swamp forest is beginning to reestablish itself along the marsh's southeastern edge as the salinity level of the water slowly decreases. On follow-up field surveys, Bissell has confirmed the emergence of silver maples; red, black, and pumpkin ashes; and yellow birches, the shade from which is beating back the phragmites. Even more remarkably, members of the swamp forest understory, such as swamp rose, robust smartweed, high-bush blueberry, wood reed, and weak bog sedge, are springing forth from seeds that have lain dormant in the earth where the now-retreating phragmites once choked off light and nourishment. Appreciation for the ecosystem's resilience must be added to understanding of its significance.

The perception of many nearby residents that Mentor Marsh was nothing more than a mosquito breeding ground lingered well into the 1970s. However, as Mentor evolved from a rural community notable for its many nurseries into a densely built town of more than fifty thousand served by numerous large shopping centers, sentiment changed. Disappearance of open space in Lake County was a growing cause for concern, and the entire Mentor Marsh ecosystem has become a source of pride and a rallying point for a loose coalition of preservation-minded individuals and institutions in Lake County. Many of these forces supported the city of Mentor's lagoons conservation initiative in 1996.

Four years earlier, Mentor City Council and administration had convened a working group consisting of representatives of various regional organizations and concerned residents to discuss the future of the lagoons property. A court-ordered receivership had called for the liquidation of 380 acres. After doing its homework—making site visits, consulting with dozens of local and state agencies, and having the parcel appraised—the working group prepared a plan that outlined various scenarios for acquiring the property and identified possible funding sources. (A grant from The Cleveland Foundation supported the planning effort.) When it became clear that no other public body was willing or able to take the lead and that the only potential private partners were interested solely in building homes on the land, the city made the commitment to going it alone. Having determined to cover the cost of acquiring the lagoons property at fair market value by issuing bonds that could be paid off over twenty years (from anticipated income tax revenues), Mentor's city administration submitted a bid to the court in 1995.

End of story? Not quite.

Crying halt. The city of Mentor's determination to acquire the lagoons property prevented developers from turning this rare lake plain habitat into yet another subdivision.

At this point the decades-long battle over the future of this peerless landscape escalated. Unwilling to accept defeat, and utilizing public records to their advantage, private development interests offered the court a higher bid for the parcel, which included the marina and sections of upland forest, marsh, and beach. The court accepted Blue Heron Ltd.'s offer. Having come this far, the city of Mentor refused to yield. Defying a hailstorm of local newspaper stories and editorials in favor of private ownership, Mentor City Council passed a resolution in April 1996 to acquire the lagoons through eminent domain. A handful of pro-development advocates forced a referendum seeking voter approval of the city's eminent domain action; this referendum appeared on the November 1996 ballot.

Under the banner of the Mentor Lagoons Preservation Committee begun by residents Ron and Judy Prosek, Clem and Evelyn Kiffmeyer, and Bill and Carolyn Wetzel, volunteers mailed flyers and went from door to door and from block to block, encouraging voters to support the city's conservation initiative. By a vote of 11,533 to 8,583, 57 percent of the voters favored the acquisition. The developers finally yielded, agreeing in a court-negotiated settlement to sell the property to the city of Mentor for $9 million in the summer of 1997. That fall Mentor City Council voted to acquire an additional seventy acres of adjacent upland forest; city manager Julian M. Suso had personally negotiated the land purchase with a few private owners sympathetic to the city's desire to ensure the preservation of significant

Day's end. Revenues generated by the city's operation of a formerly private marina at the lagoons have helped to pay off Mentor's bond obligations on the entire property.

sections of upland forest and beach. Ten of those key acres formerly belonged to one of the developers, who had quietly purchased the lakefront parcel for the construction of his own eight-thousand-square-foot home. Through the city's efforts, work was finally halted after the structure's foundation was built, when the courts ruled that the developer could not recoup his building costs should the city prevail in its eminent domain action to acquire the parcel. Today the imposing concrete foundation remains a sobering testament to the fate that would have befallen the entire lagoons property had not the city of Mentor come to its rescue.

A year after the referendum, Mentor residents returned to the polls to approve an amendment to the city's charter that provides further protection of Mentor Lagoons Nature Preserve and Marina. The amendment requires city council to seek the voters' approval before it authorizes major alterations to these public lands. Actions that have been taken by the city's Department of Parks, Recreation, and Public Lands include making electrical repairs and improving services by providing golf carts for those unable to explore the preserve on foot. Marina revenues generated in the first thirty months of city operation have covered operating expenses and paid for half of the city's annual bond obligation that financed this acquisition.

Every year, the Ohio Lake Erie Commission, a governmental agency created in 1992 by then governor George V. Voinovich to coordinate state efforts to restore Lake Erie, presents awards recognizing work of outstanding benefit to the fourth largest of the Great Lakes. In 1999 the city of Mentor received the Ohio Lake Erie Commission Award, a fitting recognition of the determined effort that saved a singular piece of the state's lakefront for public enjoyment.

In accepting the award, city manager Suso described the preservation of the lagoons as "nothing short of a miracle—the pressures for growth and development are profound." Thanks to the precedent set in Mentor, the next time a community desires to preserve needed open space or to protect an important habitat, it may not require a "miracle." As Mentor demonstrated for the first time in Ohio's history, visionary public officials, acting on behalf of an enlightened electorate, can use eminent domain as a tool not only to promote development, but to protect us from it.

UPPER DOAN VALLEY PARKLANDS

Restoring "God's Pleasure"

SHAKER HEIGHTS/CLEVELAND HEIGHTS

The North Union Shaker Community thought of the upper reaches of Doan Brook as the "Valley of God's Pleasure." Looking for a harmonious retreat in which to practice their belief in communal living, pacifism, and celibacy and to sustain themselves as farmers and craftspeople, the members of the nineteenth-century religious group settled on 1,366 acres fed by the pristine stream. Something akin to that feeling of awe for the riches of the upper Doan Valley overtakes those who retrace the Shakers' footsteps a century after the colony sold its land holdings, abandoned its sixty community buildings, and drifted away. Hemmed in on both sides by rushing traffic and mile after mile of well-appointed homes, the section of the Doan Brook watercourse that lies between present-day Shaker Heights, Ohio, and University Circle in Cleveland is an unexpected, almost otherworldly corridor of green in a busy suburban setting.

Where else in Greater Cleveland can you find a pocket cattail marsh bounded by three city streets? Stop by the marsh on a summer day. Listen to the whir of crickets and the wind rustling in the cottonwoods. Watch the darting of dragonflies and the swoop of a red-winged blackbird. You would swear you were in the country, not standing on the border of Shaker Heights and Cleveland Heights.

The Shaker dam at Horseshoe Lake. The sylvan site of a nineteenth-century woolen mill operated by the North Union Shaker Community now serves the recreational needs of Cleveland's busy Heights suburbs.

It is equally hard to imagine that Doan Brook, nourisher of this and other vital habitats, begins as an anonymous trickle somewhere in suburban Shaker Heights. On the first leg of its nine-mile journey to Lake Erie, Doan Brook passes through culverts and front-yard drainage ditches. The rivulet barely makes its presence known. That is, until you come upon the Shaker Lakes, one of Greater Cleveland's most famous riparian landscapes. The lake district owes its natural charm to artifice: It wasn't God's pleasure but humankind that created the picturesque Horseshoe Lake and the Lower Shaker Lake, the oldest artificial body of water in Ohio.

The Lower Lake materialized in 1829 when the Shakers dammed Doan Brook to create a power source for a gristmill. The colony's desire for a woolen mill produced Horseshoe Lake in 1852. Girdled by paths, the Shaker Lakes district is a sylvan haven for joggers, walkers, and nature lovers. The flora and fauna found in and around the lakes range from fathead minnows to snapping turtles, mallards to muskrats, chives to water lilies. The parklands are also a fascinating archeological site containing known and possibly hidden Shaker ruins that the city of Shaker Heights, in collaboration with the Shaker Historical Society and the Garden Club of Cleveland, is working to document and make more accessible to the public. Plans are underway, for example, to clear the overgrowth from the foundation of the Lower Lake sawmill, which lies hidden at the bottom of a steep grade near the southeast corner of

Lower Lake. The Upper Doan Valley, embracing two Shaker-built lakes, is perhaps Greater Cleveland's most famous riparian landscape.

North Park Boulevard and Coventry Road. Educational signage will be installed to explain the site's historic significance, and the area will be relandscaped with native plants.

The Shaker Lakes are surely the best-known feature of the upper Doan Valley, a natural concourse with a 279-acre core donated to Cleveland by the Shaker Heights Land Company in 1896. In the less frequently patronized stretch of the parklands west of Coventry Road between Fairhill Road and North Park Boulevard, the terrain grows wilder and more dramatic. It is here that Doan Brook begins its descent from the Heights into University Circle. As the grade of the land steepens, the stream gains speed and power. Since its formation during the last ice age, Doan Brook has carved a deep, narrow gorge in the Portage Escarpment, the cliff that marks the dividing line between the Appalachian Plateaus and the Central Lowlands throughout the state and, in Cleveland, gives the Heights its name.

At a point across from the intersection of Kemper Road and Fairhill, the gorge is fully fifty feet high from stream bed to embankment. So thick and tangled is the vegetation along the parkway, it is a safe bet that only a relative handful of the tens of thousands of commuters who buzz past the gorge twice each workday are aware of the presence of this "giant slice of time."

The colorful description of Doan Brook gorge comes from an influential study of the Shaker Lakes parklands conducted by the National Audubon Society in 1966. The study was

Vital habitat. In its upper reaches, Doan Brook nourishes a pocket cattail marsh.

commissioned by the Shaker Lakes Garden Club, whose members used the Audubon findings to rally decisive public opposition to the county's plans to build intersecting eight-lane freeways on top of the Shaker Lakes. Challenging the view of Cuyahoga County engineer Albert S. Porter, who maintained that modern roadways were more important than a "dinky park and two-bit duck pond," the Audubon study declared the Doan Brook parkway to be an incomparable outdoor classroom. Here one could study nature (the parkway's sixty species of wildflowers, say, or its two hundred-plus species of nesting and migratory birds); appreciate local history (in particular, the earth and stone dams that "stand as mute witnesses to the skills and resourcefulness of the Shakers"); and see geological forces at work in the gorge.

In carving out this deep channel, Doan Brook exposed veins of various sedimentary rocks deposited several hundred million years ago when the Great Lakes region was an inland sea. The massive vertical face on the north side of the stream near Roxboro Road is Berea sandstone, for example. Downstream, one sees that Doan Brook has cut down to and through older deposits of reddish-brown Bedford shale and Euclid bluestone (a hard, fine-grained sandstone much prized at the turn of the century by the city's affluent home builders). Farther downstream, where the watercourse changes to a more northerly direction as it travels over the Portage Escarpment, still-older veins of Cleveland shale and the underlying Chagrin shale may be seen, especially if you are in the company of a knowledgeable and sharp-eyed guide. Naturalists say that there are few other spots in the region where so many distinct layers of the earth's crust can be viewed in so compact an area.

The gorge harbors other interesting sights. In 1844 the North Union Shakers built a gristmill into the north face of the gorge across from the present-day Kemper Road. The multi-story mill, tall and narrow as a skyscraper and said to be a marvel of engineering, served local farmers for about forty years. Sometime before the disbandment of the Shaker colony (its ranks had dwindled from three hundred strong in the 1850s to one-tenth that number by the late 1880s), the mill site was leased to an entrepreneur named Charles Reader. Reader was more interested in quarrying stone than in grinding corn and wheat, so he decided to rid himself of the imposing sandstone structure. To celebrate the Fourth of July in 1886 he stuffed it with dynamite and struck a match.

On a Sunday afternoon 114 years later, a group of fifty or so curious souls scrambles down the north embankment of Doan Brook to look at what little remains of the gristmill. They perch in knots of two and three on a rock ledge, peering down at a square notch cut into the wall of the gorge. The notch once secured one of the timbers used to dam the brook above the gristmill. Then it's on to an abandoned stone quarry, the entrance to which lies down a flight of wide stone stairs across from the intersection of Delaware Drive and North Park. The stairs inspire a round of speculation. Are they a remnant of the original landscaping of the parklands designed by E. W. Bowditch of Boston? Or are they a Works Progress Administration improvement? Even the guides from the Nature Center at Shaker Lakes do not know the answer.

The hidden grotto is dark, labyrinthine, and silent as a tomb. Hundred-year-old graffiti cover its stone walls. As the group winds its way out of the quarry area and down a long, steep incline to the slick stream bed lined with sedimentary slabs, the sound of gently flowing water becomes audible. Here, at last, one finds the Doan Brook that must have seduced Nathaniel Doane. A Connecticut blacksmith who was a member of Moses Cleaveland's second surveying party, Doane returned with his family to the Western Reserve and in 1799 decided to settle near the stream. Here, in the western end of the gorge, Doan Brook is the gently burbling stream set in deep woods that its namesake must have found as pretty as a picture.

"Right now the water in the brook is flowing at ten cubic feet per second," notes one of

Who knew? West of Coventry Road, Doan Brook gorge shelters the remains of a nineteenth-century stone quarry.

the Nature Center guides, a sandy-haired man in his early twenties. Established in 1966 as another positive outcome of the Audubon study, the Nature Center has organized the early fall hike as part of an ongoing campaign to increase public awareness and appreciation of Doan Brook. "During a hundred-year rainstorm," the guide continues, "the volume of water in the channel would increase to 9,000 c.f.s." To help the group appreciate the dimensions of such a surge, the Nature Center staff member likens a cubic foot of water to a basketball. "The amount of runoff flowing through here during the worst storm of the century," he explains, "would be the equivalent of 9,000 basketballs passing by your face every second."

Recognized by the U.S. Department of the Interior as a National Environmental Education Landmark in 1971, the Nature Center has become a leading authority on the history, attributes, contributions, and problems of this urban stream. (Be on the lookout for a Doan Brook handbook the center is preparing, which will share this expertise.) Like most of Greater Cleveland's waterways, Doan Brook has been seriously affected by pollution. Industrial waste is typically a culprit, but not in this case. Phosphorus, nitrogen, and contaminants found in Doan Brook and the Shaker Lakes come from the households, lawns, and cars of the 145,000 people who live in the 7,500-acre watershed. Pollutants such as detergents, oil, pesticides, fertilizers, grass clippings, pet waste, automobile fluids, and road salts are swept into the watershed by sewer overflows and storm runoff, which have increased in

Restoring "God's Pleasure"

Stewards of the watershed. Unlike most polluted urban streams, Doan Brook has a diverse and loyal group of supporters who have championed its cleanup for more than twenty-five years.

volume and velocity as the amount of impervious surface in the watershed nears 30 percent. As a consequence, the Doan Brook watershed suffers from degraded water quality and loss of plant, aquatic, and animal life. The upper and lower lakes periodically silt in. And, all too frequently, flooding of the watercourse stalls traffic on Martin Luther King, Jr., Drive and threatens valuable educational and cultural properties in University Circle.

Unlike most small urban streams, however, Doan Brook is lucky to have found champions: the stewards of the upper Doan Valley parklands. Recognizing that responsible park management in this instance requires them to be environmental activists, representatives of the city of Cleveland, the municipalities of Shaker Heights and Cleveland Heights (which maintain the Shaker Lakes parklands under long-term lease agreements with Cleveland), and the Nature Center at Shaker Lakes meet regularly under the auspices of the Joint Committee on the Doan Brook Watershed. Other members of the ad hoc planning body have included volunteers from the League of Women Voters, area garden clubs, and private industry, as well as professionals from concerned agencies such as the Northeast Ohio Regional Sewer District, University Circle, Inc., the Cuyahoga County Board of Health, and the Northeast Ohio Areawide Coordinating Agency. Although it has no taxing authority, the Joint Committee has tried to promote plans to monitor and improve water quality, prevent flooding, and protect habitats throughout the watershed. Members also collaborate on projects

Budding ecologists. Children enjoy an environmental education program at the Nature Center at Shaker Lakes.

aimed at enhancing public enjoyment of this natural resource. "We've accomplished a lot through cooperation," notes Jan Devereaux, a member of both the committee and the Shaker Heights City Council.

Like the return of the frogs.

The Joint Committee on the Doan Brook Watershed grew out of an attempt in the early 1970s to explain some puzzling phenomena observed by the staff and clientele of the Nature Center, which had built headquarters on South Park Boulevard in 1969 in order to carry out its mission of preserving the Shaker Lakes and providing suburban children and adults with opportunities to study and enjoy this natural area. People were curious: "Why does the Lower Lake silt in so rapidly?" and "Where have all the frogs gone?" and "Is it *really* true that our sewers drain into Doan Brook?" (An enterprising Heights teacher helped to demonstrate the veracity of this "rumor" by handing out Ping-Pong balls to her students, with instructions to flush them down their toilets at home. Sure enough, the balls popped up later in the brook.) Deciding to add environmental education and action to its agenda, the Nature Center teamed with the newly formed Shaker Lakes Water Quality Committee to sponsor a study of the Lower Lake aimed at determining what was causing its rapid sedimentation and why it harbored so few life forms other than goldfish and carp.

Concerned by the study's findings, in early 1974 the center and the committee sponsored a public symposium on the environmental degradation of Doan Brook; held at the Cleveland Museum of Natural History, it opened many eyes. The symposium paved the way for an application for a federal demonstration grant to clean up the stream. In recent years the Joint Committee has expanded its focus to include the health of the entire watershed. Joint Committee consciousness-raising has spurred interventions that have improved the water quality of Doan Brook enough to support a greater diversity of aquatic life. Green frogs, wood frogs, and bullfrogs can once again be spotted in and around the Shaker Lakes.

In 1998, one of the Joint Committee partners, the Northeast Ohio Regional Sewer District (manager of three major wastewater treatment plants serving fifty-two suburban communities and the city of Cleveland), accelerated the remediation effort by applying for a massive infusion of federal funds. It received monies to undertake a comprehensive $4.2 million study aimed at developing a long-term, systemic plan for managing the watershed's interrelated sanitary sewer, flooding, and water-quality problems. While the study was underway, the Sewer District made resources available to a broad range of independent improvement projects including technical training for municipalities in state-of-the-art stormwater management practices, experiments with biofilters and bioengineering, and public education programs. Public education is perhaps the most important component of a long-term watershed management plan. Remember the adage from the 1960s: If you aren't part of the solution, you're part of the problem? Average citizens must be educated about how their personal practices can help—or hurt—Doan Brook.

With an initial grant from the sewer district and additional support from the George Gund Foundation and the Holden Trust, the Nature Center at Shaker Lakes has taken on this particularly daunting challenge with enthusiasm. Under visionary director Nancy King Smith, the center mounted a kickoff "Year of the Brook" that began on Earth Day 1998.

Upper Doan Valley Parklands

Stream doctor. The Nature Center encourages volunteers to perform simple but regular water-quality tests at their favorite spots along the brook and to share the results with staff.

Timed to celebrate the bicentennial of the Doane family's settlement in the vicinity of Euclid Avenue and East 107th Street, Year of the Brook activities offered a little something for everyone. A costumed "Nathaniel Doane" made the rounds of schools and community groups, sharing the history and lore of Doan Brook. The Nature Center refocused its course offerings for schoolchildren and adult learners around watershed issues. It invited the public to an ice cream social held streamside in Rockefeller Park, during which Lolley the Trolley gave sightseeing tours of the Doan Brook parklands. The ice cream social proved so popular, it was repeated in 2000. Other recent programming innovations include four-season "Brook Walks" and summer concerts "By the Brook" in Rockefeller Park.

The Nature Center's director and staff realize that it is not enough to invite people to enjoy Doan Brook. They must also promote environmental stewardship of the watershed.

"We want people to realize that when they dump paint down the drain in their garages," Nancy King Smith observes, "it shows up later in the brook as pink or purple splotches." Visitors to the Nature Center are encouraged to become "Stream Doctors," picking out a spot on the brook, keeping it free of litter, and performing simple but regular water-quality tests, the results of which are recorded and shared with staff. "Street Artists" are given the tools to stencil a cautionary message—"Dump No Waste, Drains To Brook"—on storm drains in their neighborhoods. Nature Center staff members stand ready to advise home-owners on simple technologies they can employ in their own backyards to control storm water runoff.

"Use low-phosphorus lawn fertilizer," they counsel. "Pick up pet waste. You might even think about growing grass on your garage roof." Behavior modification may not be tradi-tional parks programming, but it will clearly be required if Greater Clevelanders intend to fully restore God's pleasure in the Doan Brook Valley.

EPILOGUE

Envisioning a Brighter, Greener Future

Northeast Ohio has long been blessed with significant holdings of parklands. These include the Cleveland Lakefront State Park, Cleveland's inner ring of large municipal parks, Cleveland Metroparks, and other multi-unit metropolitan park districts throughout the eight-county area. In the past we have tended to view these large oases of green as independent entities. Indeed, we may have thought that parks located more than a few miles from our homes belonged to "someone else."

No longer. A parks and recreation *network* is taking shape in northeast Ohio that will promote the interconnectivity of people throughout the region with one another and with the riches of this particular place. When more fully evolved, the network will link parks and green spaces throughout northeast Ohio, offering urbanites and suburbanites easier and greater access to nature and wildlife, to recreational resources in all parts of the network, to alternative means of traveling to and from network destinations, and to attractions and events that illuminate the region's fascinating history and cultural assets. In physically bringing together people from all walks of life, the network will help to unite us socially. It will even provide tools for neighborhood renewal, community building, and economic development.

A major impetus behind the creation of our emerging regional parks and recreation network is the Ohio & Erie Canal National Heritage Corridor, a green "Empowerment Zone," if you will, encompassing the historic canal lands that lie between Cleveland and New Philadelphia, Ohio. Eventually neighborhoods and cities throughout the region, and the parks and attractions to which they are home, will be linked to the 110-mile-long Heritage Corridor via hiking and biking paths, scenic parkways, or excursion rail line—or through related leisure programming and commerce.

At the heart of CanalWay Ohio (as the corridor is also called) is the Cuyahoga Valley National Park, at 33,000 acres the largest open space in the region. Sheltering a rich diversity of natural and cultural landscapes, the national park (formerly known as the Cuyahoga Valley National Recreation Area) is threaded by the longest completed stretch of the Towpath Trail. This twenty-mile-long ribbon of crushed limestone is the central hiking and biking path of the emerging regional parks and recreation network. Already on the books are more than thirty proposals for spur trails and bikeways that will one day connect people in all corners of northeast Ohio to CanalWay via the Towpath Trail.

Ideally, most of us in the area will be able to gain entrée to the regional parks network within walking distance of our homes. The public-private partners who are inventing the network, component by component, believe that no neighborhood or community should go unserved and unconnected. To achieve this objective, parks proponents must move decisively on a number of fronts.

They must work to re-adapt open space that already exists in our neighborhoods, such as school playgrounds, corner wood lots, tree lawns, median strips, and even such unlikely spots as large parking lots, rooftops, and industrial brownfields. One need look no farther than the ParkWorks initiative featured earlier in these pages, which is seeking to fund and build safe, well-equipped play areas and learning gardens for student and adult use in more than sixty Cleveland neighborhoods, to find a convincing demonstration of the socio-economic value of even small-scale reclamation projects. The Cuyahoga County Planning Commission has taken the lead in preparing a master plan of similar opportunities, strategies, and possible financing mechanisms for "re-greening" Greater Cleveland. While the political will to execute this comprehensive plan is still coalescing in municipalities throughout the county, the Cuyahoga County Commissioners have committed $375,000 to the advancement of the re-greening initiative.

Elsewhere, various community groups, especially in Cleveland and its inner-ring suburbs, are already working to realize their own dreams of a brighter, greener future. The limitations of space permit only a partial listing of the intriguing possibilities:

A lockkeeping demonstration in the Ohio & Erie Canal National Heritage Corridor. Federal recognition of the canal, a nearly intact example of nineteenth-century transportation technology, is opening the gates to greater economic growth throughout the region.

- In the aftermath of a devastating fire that destroyed the largely vacant Worsted Mills factory complex in Cleveland's North Broadway/East 55th Historic District, Slavic Village Development Corporation has partnered with the Boys and Girls Clubs of Cleveland, a social service agency for inner-city children, to plan a new headquarters and create much-needed athletic fields on the brownfield. A raised-grade bikeway—to be built along the old Wheeling & Lake Erie Railroad track that bisects the former industrial site—would meander through this dense urban neighborhood before connecting with the Mill Creek Falls Park & Trail featured earlier in these pages.

- Taking its lead from residents who spontaneously gather on "Tremont Ridge" during the summer months to view the fireworks at Jacobs Field (the home of the Cleveland Indians), Tremont West Development Corporation plans to convert this narrow strip of

Envisioning a Brighter, Greener Future

land along University Road into a linear park affording unparalleled views of downtown Cleveland and the northern industrial valley.

- Nearby, Train Avenue may become the site of a proposed central-city industrial parkway that will offer workers an unusual perk: easy access to CanalWay via a new hike/bike trail.

- Eco-City Cleveland, an environmental education and advocacy organization, is teaming with the Detroit-Shoreway Community Development Organization to develop a model "green village" that will (among other things) seek to enhance the open-space potential of the urban streetscape, including such typically mundane places as a new rapid transit stop at Madison Avenue and West 65th Street.

- In Parma, voters, responding favorably to a grass-roots campaign led by resident David Vasarhelyi, approved a $3 million bond issue to purchase 100-plus acres of woodlands along West Creek, a tributary of the Cuyahoga River. This still-wild place had long been eyed for commercial and residential development. Since expanded to 260 acres, with plans for additional growth under discussion, West Creek Preserve and Greenway is already providing suburbanites in Parma, Seven Hills, Brooklyn Heights, and Independence with welcome new opportunities for outdoor recreation literally in their own backyards.

- The Friends of Whiskey Island, an ad hoc group led by steelworker Ed Hauser, is championing the reclamation of this triangular peninsula in the mouth of the Cuyahoga River as a public park. First inhabited by early settler Lorenzo Carter and later by Irish immigrants (who abandoned the land to the railroads, a salt mine, and the Hulett iron ore unloaders in the twentieth century), the parcel is rich in history and natural beauty. It is also home to a nationally recognized, late art deco former U.S. Coast Guard station (the work of J. Milton Dyer, the local architect who designed Cleveland City Hall and the Cleveland Athletic Club). The proposed Whiskey Island park will continue to afford the public much-needed access to the lakefront and unrivaled views of the downtown skyline.

- Dike 14, the eighty-eight-acre landfill at the northern end of Gordon Park, has long been intended for park development. The John P. Murphy Foundation has underwritten a study by Behnke Associates, the Cleveland landscape architects, of the feasibility of building a lakefront sculpture park there. Mobilized by the late civic leader and philanthropist Herbert E. Strawbridge, proponents of the new sculpture park believe that it would enhance the preeminence of the parklands straddling Martin Luther King, Jr., Boulevard as a venue for public art. A coalition of local nature and environmental organizations is recommending that the site, which abounds with bird and plant life, be turned into a nature preserve.

Epilogue

- Proponents of *Civic Vision 2000 and Beyond,* a master plan for the city of Cleveland, have recommended that the eight-lane Inner Belt be converted into a six-lane, reduced-speed parkway (like Chicago's Lakeshore Boulevard) from Deadman's Curve to East 9th Street. In itself a welcome improvement, the reconfiguration might have the ancillary benefit of freeing land needed to complete Cleveland's long-discussed lakefront bikeway. A $7.2 million study to determine the Inner Belt's future, funded by the Ohio Department of Transportation, began in January 2001.

An abundance of open spaces in congested urban settings is a critical component of the emerging regional parks and recreational network. There is an equally urgent need for preservation of outlying open space—farmland, natural areas, and rural and semirural settings that readily distinguish Greater Cleveland from other, denser metropolitan areas. This "middle landscape" of cornfields, orchards, creeks, and small towns, which is as integral to our regional identity and well-being as roaring coke ovens, is disappearing at an alarming rate. To illustrate the degree to which urban sprawl is overtaking the region: In Geauga County, nearly fifty-five thousand acres of open land were converted to commercial and residential use between 1975 and 1996. In the last two years the pace of development in Geauga has quickened, outstripping the rate at which land is being preserved ten to one. Similar trends can be seen throughout the region.

Recognizing that park creation can be one (although not the only) mechanism for controlling encroaching development, managers of eight metropolitan park districts in the region are now meeting regularly in an attempt to define what park districts can do individually and collectively to preserve, enhance, and connect the most important natural areas that remain untouched. The Park Districts Open Space Committee was convened in 1997 by Lake County Metroparks deputy director Stephen W. Madewell, who was spurred to take this action by the widespread but erroneous assumption that the metropolitan park districts alone would be capable of solving the region's land management problems. Using GIS (Geographic Information Systems) technology fine tuned and made available by Cleveland Metroparks, the Open Space Committee prepared a comprehensive inventory of open land in the cooperating park districts' respective service areas. Armed with this data, elected officials, urban planners and policy makers can now identify—across jurisdictional boundaries—key natural areas and open spaces in northeast Ohio that should be kept forever green. At a fall 2001 conference, the metropolitan park districts announced that they are primed to advance the conservation effort by helping communities to assess options for acquiring or conserving desirable land, to analyze the cost of open-space protection initiatives, and to explore possible methods of financing.

Finally, the regional parks movement must capitalize on the potential of the Heritage Corridor to become a recreational resource and tourist draw comparable to Colonial Williamsburg, the Blue Ridge Parkway, and the Appalachian Trail all rolled into one. Here is how that can be done.

When Congress designated the Ohio & Erie Canal as a National Heritage Corridor in 1996, it conferred more than national prestige and attention on this priceless artifact of America's westward expansion. With this recognition comes seed monies from the U.S. Department of the Interior to help corridor communities preserve and promote their historic, cultural, and recreational resources in order to achieve greater social and economic benefits. Over the next several years, the Ohio & Erie Canal National Heritage Corridor Committee, a regional oversight body, will distribute these funds in accordance with a master management plan for CanalWay that was adopted in the fall of 2000. If all goes according to plan, $10 million in seed money is expected to leverage approximately $150 million in enhancements that will showcase the wealth of natural, recreational, historic, and cultural assets within the corridor in a compelling and coordinated fashion. As its tag line proclaims, CanalWay proponents are intent on "building a new kind of park."

A key improvement will be the development of alternative means of navigating the corridor. The plan anticipates the day when the Towpath Trail will extend the full length of CanalWay, and the Cuyahoga Valley Scenic Railroad can be boarded in downtown Cleveland and taken as far as the pre-canal settlement of Zoar in Tuscarawas County. (The railroad currently offers excursions between Independence and Akron, with a stop in Peninsula, the former canal boomtown.) Coordinated maps, highway markers, interpretive waysides, and rest areas will enhance CanalWay's designation as a National Scenic Byway, enabling those who prefer to travel by car to find their way easily to the corridor's natural beauty spots, historic buildings and sites, recreational facilities, and cultural attractions.

To complement existing sources of information about particular sites, three CanalWay Centers will tell the story of how the canal shaped the region as a whole. These visitor centers—in Cleveland, Akron, and Zoar—will also serve as major gateways to CanalWay, providing orientation for sightseeing trips to its hundreds of "heritage venues": individual buildings of architectural or historic merit, archeological sites, small preserved villages, rural and agricultural landscapes, scenic natural features, interesting wildlife and plant habitats, distinctive neighborhoods and urban areas, and significant industrial settings.

To be located in sizable new parks, CanalWay Centers will be attractions in their own right. For example, Canal Basin Park, the $35 million visitors center planned for the northern terminus of the Ohio & Erie Canal, will display interpretive exhibits in an iconic setting: a restored Baltimore & Ohio Railroad station. The juxtaposition of this historic building with the nearby, rewatered turning basin, where crews once repositioned canal boats for the return journey south, will give visitors a vivid picture of two transportation innovations that fueled the region's growth. It is possible that two decommissioned Hulett iron-ore unloaders—rare examples of a technology developed in Cleveland that were saved from the scrap heap by an eleventh-hour fund-raising campaign led by citizen activists—will be reassembled in the park near an earthen-ore boat. If so, they will serve as fascinating symbols of the Great Lakes shipping industry, another transportation mode critical to the region's economic development.

The Ohio & Erie Canal Association, the corridor's management agency, is spearheading the development of the CanalWay Centers, as well as providing technical and financial assistance to heritage venues interested in optimizing their appeal by building physical linkages to the corridor; improving their facilities or conserving green space; developing coordinated displays, interpretive materials, and programming; or undertaking new marketing initiatives. Staffed by the Ohio Canal Corridor, the Ohio & Erie Canal Corridor Coalition, and Cuyahoga Valley National Park, the not-for-profit management agency understands that the more venues that participate in corridor programs, the more attractive a destination CanalWay becomes.

Because it is rich in parks, situated near Lake Erie and blessed with forty major cultural attractions ranging from the Art Museum in Cleveland to Blossom Music Center in Cuyahoga Falls and from Stan Hywet Hall and Gardens in Akron to the Pro Football Hall of Fame in Canton, northeast Ohio is already a major recreational destination, attracting an estimated 16.5 million visitors annually. CanalWay could position the region to capture an even greater share of the nation's travel and leisure business, a sector that is poised to become the No. 1

industry in the United States, according to the National Park Service. Implementation of the corridor master plan is expected to increase visitation in the area by approximately 20 percent. That translates into some 3.3 million more tourists pouring into northeast Ohio annually.

As a focal point for projected additional annual leisure-time expenditures of $69 million, CanalWay has the potential to be a powerful engine of economic development. When more fully realized, it will create jobs and businesses aimed at satisfying demand for new recreational amenities and visitor-oriented services. It will boost property values and inspire investment in neighborhoods and communities that shelter heritage venues. And, because professionals weighing competing job offers, and businesses deciding where to build or relocate, are heavily influenced by their perceptions of the quality of life offered by the cities under consideration, CanalWay could be an important new recruitment tool for the region, as well.

CanalWay proponents believe that the regional redevelopment project, in addition to spurring our economy, will lift our civic spirits. By highlighting the accomplishments of the entrepreneurs, captains of industry, and blue-collar workers who together created much of the region's wealth, CanalWay could indeed nourish feelings of solidarity and pride among northeast Ohioans from all walks of life. Economic prosperity, in turn, made it possible for each segment of the community to make its own distinctive contributions, enriching the quality of life for all. The civic spirit that inspired three of the city's wealthy industrialists to give away the land that became Wade, Rockefeller, and Gordon Parks burned just as brightly in the hearts of the thousands of now-anonymous individuals who poured their hard-earned nickels and dimes into the creation of Cleveland's internationally unparalleled Cultural Gardens. If CanalWay succeeds in making plain the social, cultural, and economic interdependence of all those who live in northeast Ohio, it will likely spur other kinds of regional planning efforts and collaborations whose far-reaching benefits we can only begin to imagine.

Outsiders may also begin to look at us differently. CanalWay—and related green development envisioned for neighborhoods and communities all along the Ohio & Erie Canal National Heritage Corridor—affords us a real opportunity to turn the region's unflattering "rust-belt" label on its head. By making our economic history and industrial infrastructure an integral part of an ever-expanding but cohesive regional parks network, Greater Clevelanders will be declaring emphatically that we are proud of who we are and what we have

Year-round pleasure. The Doan Brook parklands are frequented by nature lovers and exercise seekers even in winter.

accomplished. A celebration of the unique character and strengths of this region could put an end to our difficulties in projecting a favorable image to the rest of the nation.

What will it take to achieve this monumental vision and reap its benefits?

To restore and upgrade our existing green spaces, create new parks and recreational resources at both the neighborhood and regional levels, and undertake legacy projects of the magnitude of a Canal Basin Park will take a significant, but not insurmountable, public investment. Funding of at least $200 to $250 million—in other words, a commitment roughly equivalent to the outlay for a new baseball stadium for the Cleveland Indians *and* the renovation of the Cleveland Orchestra's Severance Hall—will be required. Dogged civic leadership (of the type demonstrated seventy-five years ago by the strong-willed women of the Garden Club of Cleveland, who took it upon themselves to create a suitable garden setting for the Cleveland Museum of Art when no one else could be motivated to improve the appearance of the museum's weedy construction site) will be an equally critical element in moving a comprehensive parks agenda forward.

Even more important will be the expenditure of political capital. Clearly, one or more of northeast Ohio's most powerful elected officials must be willing to step forward as passionate advocates for the vision. The ideal champions would possess the rhetorical skills of a Sherwood Anderson, the twentieth-century novelist who celebrated life in small-town Ohio, and the political acumen of a John Seiberling or a Ralph Regula, the congressional leaders who pushed hard for the creation of the Cuyahoga Valley National Park and the Ohio & Erie Canal National Heritage Corridor, respectively. Elected leaders must use their bully pulpits to explain and endorse the concept of building an interconnected regional parks network, articulate its life-enriching possibilities, and lobby hard for the necessary public funding.

Although ambitious green development projects are underway elsewhere in the country —some also inspired by official "Heritage Corridor" designations—no other proposed park-building effort surpasses that envisioned for northeast Ohio in scale and impact. If we choose to marshal the kinds of public-private partnerships applauded in this book in support of CanalWay and its many related neighborhood redevelopment initiatives, the day may come when this much-maligned region of the country is instead widely regarded, and even envied, for its exceptional parks.

FURTHER READING

Chapman, Edmund H. *Cleveland: Village to Metropolis; A Case Study of Problems of Urban Development in Nineteenth-Century America.* 2d ed. Cleveland: Western Reserve Historical Society, 1981.

Cigliano, Jan. *Showplace of America: Cleveland's Euclid Avenue, 1850–1910.* Kent, Ohio: Kent State University Press, 1991.

Cockrell, Ron. *A Green Shrouded Miracle: The Administrative History of the Cuyahoga Valley National Recreational Area, Ohio.* Omaha: National Park Service, 1992.

Cramer, C. H. *Open Shelves and Open Minds: A History of the Cleveland Public Library.* Cleveland: Press of Case Western Reserve University, 1972.

"Down in the Valley: Welcome to Cleveland Metroparks' Newest Addition: The Ohio & Erie Canal Reservation." Special section. *Cleveland Magazine,* August 1999.

Eckman, W. H., ed. *Public Parks: A Compilation of Facts and Statistics Gathered from Official and Other Sources, together with a Brief History of Park Undertakings in the United States.* Pamphlet. Cleveland: J. H. Savage, 1888.

Goulder, Grace. *John D. Rockefeller: The Cleveland Years.* Cleveland: Western Reserve Historical Society, 1972.

Holden, L. E. Address to Cleveland City Council, December 28, 1896.

Horton, John J. *The Jonathan Hale Farm: A Chronicle of the Cuyahoga Valley.* Cleveland: Western Reserve Historical Society, 1961.

Johannesen, Eric. *Cleveland Architecture, 1876–1976.* Cleveland: Western Reserve Historical Society, 1979.

Kennedy, James Harrison. *A History of the City of Cleveland: Its Settlement, Rise and Progress, 1796–1896.* Cleveland: Imperial Press, 1896.

Lederer, Clara. *Their Paths Are Peace: The Story of Cleveland's Cultural Gardens.* Cleveland: Cleveland Cultural Garden Federation, 1954.

Leedy, Walter C. Jr. *Cleveland Builds an Art Museum: Patronage, Politics, and Architecture, 1884–1916.* Cleveland: Cleveland Museum of Art, 1991.

Linking the Corridor: A Plan for the Towpath Trail in the North Cuyahoga Valley. Cleveland: Cuyahoga County Planning Commission, December 1999.

Mentor Marsh State Nature Preserve. Pamphlet. Columbus: Ohio Department of Natural Resources, n.d.

Miller, Carol Poh. *Cleveland Metroparks: Celebrating 75 Years of Conservation, Education and Recreation, 1917–1992.* Cleveland: Cleveland Metroparks, 1992.

Ohio & Erie Canal National Heritage Corridor Management Plan: Technical Report, Volume 1. Peninsula, Ohio: Ohio & Erie Canal Association, June 2000.

Orth, Samuel P. *A History of Cleveland, Ohio.* Chicago-Cleveland: S. J. Clarke Publishing Company, 1910.

The Parks of Greater Cleveland. Reprint. Cleveland: Cleveland Chamber of Commerce, August 1940.

Podojil, Catherine. "The Little Canal That Could." *Northern Ohio Live,* June 1998.

Rockefeller Park: The Future of Rockefeller Park: A Positive Statement. Cleveland: William A. Behnke Associates, 1981.

A Route to Prosperity: A Study by the National Park Service of the Ohio & Erie Canal Corridor. Omaha: National Park Service, August 1993.

Rybczynski, Witold. *A Clearing in the Distance: Frederick Law Olmsted and America in the Nineteenth Century.* New York: Scribner, 1999.

A Study and Report on City Parks, Boulevards and Playgrounds of Cleveland. Cleveland: Community Betterment Council of Cleveland, September 1923.

Van Tassel, David D., and John J. Grabowski, eds. *The Dictionary of Cleveland Biography.* Bloomington: Indiana University Press, 1996.

———. *The Encyclopedia of Cleveland History.* 2d ed. Bloomington: Indiana University Press, 1996.

Williams, Arthur B. "The Story Doan Brook Tells." Manuscript, n.d. Western Reserve Historical Society, Cleveland, Ohio.

"The World's" History of Cleveland: Commemorating the City's Centennial Anniversary. Cleveland: The Cleveland World, 1896.

Zonsius, Patricia M. *75 Years of Treasures & Pleasures: Metro Parks, Serving Summit County 1921–1996.* Pamphlet. Akron: Metro Parks, Serving Summit County, 1998.